Manuscripts

on

Purgatory

Manuscripts

on Purgatory

As Seen by Two Mystics

Sr. Marie de la Croix

St. Catherine of Genoa

Caritas Publishing

Manuscript on Purgatory. Originally published in the French bulletin *Notre Dame de la Bonne Mort* as *Le Manuscrit du Purgatoire* c.1922. Translated into English by Betty Kelly.

Treatise on Purgatory. In 1551, 41 years after her death, a book about the life and teaching of St. Catherine of Genoa was published, entitled *Libro de la vita mirabile et dottrina santa de la Beata Caterinetta de Genoa*. This is the source of her *Treatise on Purgatory*.

Republished together in this one volume *What Happens to Me After I Die?* on December 17, 2016, Traditional Feast of St. Lazarus.

ISBN: 978-1-945275-10-4

Life After Death

Those who die in God's grace and friendship and are perfectly purified live for ever with Christ. They are like God for ever, for they "see him as he is," face to face:[596] . . .

This perfect life with the Most Holy Trinity - this communion of life and love with the Trinity, with the Virgin Mary, the angels and all the blessed - is called "heaven." Heaven is the ultimate end and fulfillment of the deepest human longings, the state of supreme, definitive happiness.

To live in heaven is "to be with Christ." the elect live "in Christ,"[598] but they retain, or rather find, their true identity, their own name.[599]

> For life is to be with Christ; where Christ is, there is life, there is the kingdom.[600]

By his death and Resurrection, Jesus Christ has "opened" heaven to us. The life of the blessed consists in the full and perfect possession of the fruits of the redemption accomplished by Christ. He makes partners in his heavenly glorification those who have believed in him and remained faithful to his will. Heaven is the blessed community of all who are perfectly incorporated into Christ.

This mystery of blessed communion with God and all who are in Christ is beyond all understanding and description. Scripture speaks of it in images: life, light, peace, wedding feast, wine of the kingdom, the Father's house, the heavenly Jerusalem, paradise: "no eye has seen, nor ear heard, nor the heart of man conceived, what God has prepared for those who love him."[601]

Because of his transcendence, God cannot be seen as he is, unless he himself opens up his mystery to man's immediate contemplation and gives him the capacity for it. The Church calls this contemplation of God in his heavenly glory "the beatific vision" . . .

We cannot be united with God unless we freely choose to love him. But we cannot love God if we sin gravely against him, against our neighbor or against ourselves: "He who does not love remains in death. Anyone who hates his brother is a murderer, and you know that no murderer has eternal life abiding in him."[610] Our Lord warns us that we shall be separated from him if we fail to meet the serious needs of the poor and the little ones who are his brethren.[611] To die in mortal sin without repenting and accepting God's merciful love means remaining separated from him for ever by our own free choice. This state of definitive self-exclusion from communion with God and the blessed is called "hell" . . .

All who die in God's grace and friendship, but still imperfectly purified, are indeed assured of their eternal salvation; but after death they undergo purification, so as to achieve the holiness necessary to enter the joy of heaven.

To this final purification of the elect the Church gives the name Purgatory . . .

~ *The Catechism of the Catholic Church*
1023-1028, 1033, 1030-1031

596 1 Jn 3:2; cf. ; 1 Cor 13:12; ; Rev 22:4; 598 ; Phil 1:23; cf. ; Jn 14:3; ; 1 Thess 4:17; 599 Cf. ; Rev 2:17; 600 St. Ambrose, In Luc., 10, 121: PL 15, 1834A; 601 ; 1 Cor 2:9; 610 1 ; Jn 3:14-15; 611 Cf. ; Mt 25:31-46.

Table of Contents

Manuscript on Purgatory

Sr. Marie de la Croix

Nihil Obstat
  Rev. Msgr. Carroll E. Satterfield, S.T.D.
    Censor Librorum

Imprimatur
  ✠ His Eminence, Lawrence Cardinal Shehan
    Archbishop of Baltimore

December 26, 1967

Introduction

At the expressed desire of the Directors of the Bulletin *Notre Dame de la Bonne Mort*, this pamphlet is published with all the reservations ordered by the Church in the decree of Urban VIII, and as a purely historical document.

It was sent to that periodical by a zealous and devout missionary and is a pious document based on alleged conversations between a nun and a soul in Purgatory.

No one can deny off-hand the possibility, or in fact, the reality of such apparitions of souls in Purgatory to persons still living. Such apparitions are not rare and there are many accounts of them. They are of frequent occurrence in the lives of the Saints. We will quote only one example from the life of St. Margaret Mary Alacoque.* She says: "When I was praying before the Blessed Sacrament on the feast of Corpus Christi, a person enveloped in fire suddenly stood before me. From the pitiable state the soul was in, I knew it was in Purgatory and I wept bitterly. This soul told me it was that of a Benedictine, who had once heard my confession and ordered me to go to Holy Communion. As a reward for this, God permitted him to ask me to help him in his sufferings.

* Her *Life*, by herself, 98, 1920 edition.

"He asked me to apply to him all I should do or suffer for a period of three months. Having obtained my superior›s leave, I did what he asked. He told me that the greatest cause of his sufferings was that in life he had preferred his own interests to those of God, in that he had been too attached to his good reputation. His second defect was lack of charity to his brethren. The third was his all too natural attachment to creatures. It would be difficult for me to describe what I had to endure during those three months. He never left me and seeing him, as it were on fire and in such terrible pain, I could do nothing but groan and weep almost incessantly. My superior, being touched with compassion, told me to do hard penances, particularly to take the discipline . . . After the three months I saw the soul radiant with happiness, joy, and glory. He was about to enjoy eternal happiness, and in thanking me he said he would protect me when with God."

The testimony of theologians and of historical documents are not less numerous or convincing, but let it suffice for us to mention Canon Ribet's *Divine Mysticism*, (Vol. II, Ch. VIII) and the other outstanding works of this master of mystical theology.

God allows these apparitions and manifestations both for the relief of the souls in question who thus arouse our pity, and to instruct us by showing us the rigor of divine justice when it comes to faults which we often treat lightly. An account of several apparitions published by Msgr. Palafox y Mendosa, Bishop of Osma in Spain, bears the significant title of *Light for the Living through the Experience of the Dead*. We can hardly find better expression or vindication for such manifestations of divine providence. We must always remember that these accounts of manifestations have only a human authority. Our Holy Mother the Church has not made any pronouncement regarding them. They are treated only as historical documents.

Background of the Manuscript

This manuscript contains very interesting statements about the life beyond the grave, particularly about Purgatory. The details are intermingled with much spiritual direction. Its authenticity is beyond doubt.

A nun, identified for us merely as Sister M. de L. C.,* of a convent at V., without warning began to hear prolonged sighs beside her. This was in November 1873. She cried out, "Oh, who are you, you frighten me. Whatever you do, don't show yourself. Tell me, who are you?" No answer was forthcoming. The sighs continued and even came nearer. In vain did the poor Sister multiply her prayers, communions, ways of the cross, and rosaries. The sighs did not cease and remained unexplained until February 15, 1874, when a voice she recognized was heard saying: "Do not be afraid, you will not see me in my sufferings. I am Sister M. G." Sister M. G. was a nun who had died at V., a victim to devotion and duty, February 22, 1871, at the age of 36.

The suffering soul then told her former companion whose advice she had often despised, that she would

---

* Sr. Marie de la Croix, Augustinian nun of Valognes.

come frequently in order to help her sanctify herself. The plan of God was that Sister M. de L. C. by her holy life should relieve and ultimately deliver her, who in years past, had tried her patience so sorely. The answer did not lessen the fears of Sister M. de L. C., who requested her visitor to depart and never again return. But it was useless. She was told that she had only to bear it as long as God willed it. This was just what she dreaded. For several years the mysterious relation continued between the living nun and the departed religious. It was Sister M. de L. C., herself, who related these events from 1874 to 1890, in the manuscript which is here given to the public.

Character of the Author of this Manuscript

This is a testimonial about Sister M. de L. C. herself. All those who knew her were unanimous in declaring that she practiced all the religious virtues, even heroically. As director of a boarding school, she exercised a really supernatural influence over her pupils, who spoke of her as a saint. They said that not only her words but all of her actions impressed them more than those of any priest of their acquaintance could have done. They still live under the influence of her inspiration. Let us add that all the witnesses of her life were agreed that Sister M. de L. C. was endowed with a sound judgment, a keen and cultured intellect, and possessed of a great amount of common sense. In the spiritual life, she never sought the extraordinary. On the contrary, she avoided it.

The manuscript shows that to the very end she had doubts about what she was obligated to listen to. She often thought it was the work of the devil. It greatly annoyed her to depart from the common way of life. She wanted to be like the rest and attract no special attention. Though she was averse to the visits she received, she profited greatly by them for her own spiritual progress. Her notes of her retreats are a sufficient evidence of this. Those who saw her life and witnessed her actions are also convinced of this.

Authority of the Witnesses

In the first place it is certain that Sister M. de L. C. kept her director well informed of all that happened. He was the Reverend Father Prevel of the Fathers of Pontingy, who later became General of his congregation. The Sister's own note book shows how well she profited by her interviews with her director. A letter from him, dated November 4, 1912, sent from Hitchen, England, after a long period of separation, shows us that he was well informed on all the conversations of Sister M. de L. C. with her former companion. He writes: "Tell me about your dear suffering one, who must now be long since enjoying the glory of her Beloved. Has she abandoned you? Or does she console you in your sorrows? Have you continued writing down what she says? For my part, I have kept most carefully your former notes and have reread them many times." Clearly Father Prevel accepted the communications seriously, and we can rest assured that he had sufficient evidence for doing so.

Besides this important evidence of her director, we are fortunate in having the opinions of theologians of note, such as Canon Dubosq, superior of the Seminary of Bayeux and *Promotor Fidei* in the canonical process for the beatification and canonization of St. Therese of the Child Jesus, also Canon Gontier, diocesan *Censor Librorum*.

After examining the Manuscript carefully, these prominent priests have declared without hesitation that it contains nothing contrary to Faith, nothing that is not in accord with the true principles of the spiritual life, rather matter that will edify devout souls. They testify that Sister M. de L. C. was endowed with sound judgment and common sense and thus was protected from going astray in vivid and harmful imaginations. They were pleased at the evidence that she had done all in her power to avoid the visits, and that she protested against them, even thinking them punishments sent from heaven. She regarded the facts so strange that she did not know what to believe about them. Frequently she chided the visitor, so that she could not have imagined or invented the manifestations imposed upon her.

They were above all impressed by the great lesson of Christian charity which was manifest during the whole period of the apparitions. On the one hand Sister M. G., during her earthly life in the convent, had caused Sister M. de L. C., her spiritual guide, great suffering by her want of religious spirit and deportment. Yet it was to this very Sister that God ordered her to address herself after death, for deliverance from Purgatory. They noticed that the lights given to Sister M. de L.

C. became clearer and more distinct in proportion to Sister M. G.'s gradual purification. Finally they were impressed by the living Sister's great progress in the work of her sanctification. So remarkable was this that on reading the manuscript Canon Dubosq said, "In publishing this Manuscript, as I heartily approve, you are anticipating a cause of beatification." In a word, all theologians who were consulted gave unanimous consent that Sister M. de L. C.'s manuscript portrayed in itself proof of its authenticity, and therefore, it was of value because of both content and origin.

Conclusion

The Manuscript of Sister M. de L. C., which we will call for the sake of brevity, "The Manuscript of Purgatory," from a merely historical and human point of view seems entirely genuine and creditable.

The Directors of the magazine *Notre Dame de la Bonne Mort* are happy to be able to publish so edifying and impressive a work. A voice reaching out to us from beyond the grave makes known to us the justice and mercy of Purgatory, together with the instruction for a more perfect life of union with God, and will be helpful to many souls on their journey to eternity.

It is our hope that the "Light" made known to the living by the experience of the dead may be helpful to those seeking to lead a better life. It may even be to many of our readers a preparation for a happy death.

Manuscript on Purgatory

Our Mother Superior is in Heaven since the day of her death, thanks to her suffering and great charity.

If you were as perfect as God wishes you to be, He would be ready to bestow many graces upon you. God wants you to be holier than many others.

Father L— is in Purgatory, because he was too fond of giving retreats and preaching in many places, instead of taking care of his parish.

If you make the intention, God will accept whatever you do, for all the souls in Purgatory, just as if applied to one particular soul.

I am the one who is suffering most at the present moment, since I was not true to my vocation.

Next to the Mass, the Way of the Cross is the best prayer. Observe the strict silence well, because I often violated it. I suffer more than Sister — because she was faithful to her vocation. Suffering, however, caused her to complain, as she was badly directed spiritually. I am not able to give a visible sign. God does not permit it. I am not worthy. Because I have annoyed you so much, God wants you to pray for me. You may also tell this to

Sister — to whom I was a great source of trouble and also to Mother Superior, as I made her suffer much. Poor Reverend Mother, if only she would have some Masses offered up for me. Say a few rosaries for me and make your meditations well. I never made any. Say your divine office well. I was much distracted during mine. Observe strict religious modesty everywhere since I never kept my eyes from seeing what I should not have seen . . . Be obedient to Reverend Mother whom I annoyed so much . . .

If you could only know what I suffer! Pray for me, please. I suffer intensely everywhere. My God, how merciful You are! No one can imagine what Purgatory is like. Be kind and take pity on the poor souls . . . Do not neglect the Way of the Cross.

While on earth you will frequently suffer in body and soul, and often in both together.

It is so beautiful in Heaven. There is a great distance between Purgatory and Heaven. We are privileged at times to catch a glimpse of the joys of the blessed in Paradise, but it is almost a punishment. It makes us yearn to see God. In Heaven, it is pure delight; in Purgatory, profound darkness.

God loves you more than many others. Has He not frequently made it known to you?

Mother E— is in Heaven because she was a hidden and very spiritual soul.

No, indeed I am not the devil; I am Sister M. G. and I will try you till I am in Heaven. After that I, in my turn, will pray for you. Yes, I can pray even now and I will do so every day. You will then realize that the souls in Purgatory are not ungrateful. Those who are very guilty do not see the Blessed Virgin. It gives great joy to God when anyone is the cause of freeing a soul from Purgatory.

All you have read on this subject is true.

On Easter Sunday, I shall obtain a little relief.

If you watch carefully over yourself, God will bestow on you graces which He has never yet given to anyone else. You can offer up your office for many souls at once, if before you start the recitation, you make the intention for each soul in particular. Thus each will benefit as if you had offered it for him alone.

Purgatory is terrible for those religious who have caused trouble to their superiors. For them a special punishment is reserved similar to that which I am enduring.

March 24, 1874. Tomorrow, visit the Blessed Sacrament as often as you can. I shall accompany you. I will have the happiness of being near Our Lord. Yes, that relieves me.

March 25, 1874. I am now in the second Purgatory. Since my death, I have been in the first, where one endures such great suffering. We also suffer in the second, but not nearly as much as in the first. Always try to be a help to your superior. Do not speak often. Wait until you are questioned before you answer.

May 1874. I have been in the second Purgatory since the Feast of the Annunciation. On that day I saw the

3

Blessed Virgin for the first time. In the first stage, we never saw her. The sight of her encourages us and this beloved Mother speaks to us of Heaven. While we see her, our sufferings are greatly diminished.*

Oh, how I desire to go to Heaven! What a martyrdom we suffer once we have seen God!

What do I think? I think God permits this for your benefit and for my consolation. Listen well to what I am going to tell you. God has selected you for a special purpose. He wants you to save many souls by your advice and good example. If, by your conduct, you frustrate this, one day you will have to give an account for every soul that you could have saved. It is quite true that you are not worthy, but God permits it thus. He is the Master and distributes His graces to whomsoever He pleases.

You do well to pray to St. Michael and to urge others to do so. One is indeed happy at the hour of death when he has had confidence in some of the saints. They will be his protectors before God in that terrible moment.

Never hesitate to remind your girls of the great truths of salvation. In these days, more than ever, people need to be reminded of supernatural truths.

God wants you to sacrifice yourself for Him without reserve. He loves you more than many others, hence He will give you many more graces Be careful not to lose any of the graces that He gives you. Live only

---

* We also read that many saints and theologians say that by a special favor the Blessed Virgin sometimes shows herself to the souls in Purgatory for their relief on her feast days.

for God. Try to procure His glory everywhere. What good you can do for souls! Do nothing except what pleases God. Before each action recollect yourself for a moment to be sure that what you are going to do will be pleasing to Him. All for Jesus. Love Him well.

Yes, I suffer very much, but my greatest torment is not seeing God. It is a continuous martyrdom. It makes me suffer more than does the fire of Purgatory. If later on you love God as He wants you to, you will experience a little of the pining, which makes one long to be united to the object of one's love, to Jesus.

Yes, we sometimes see St. Joseph, but not as often as we do the Blessed Virgin.

You must become indifferent to everything except what is for God. Thus you will reach the height of perfection to which Jesus calls you.

Mother I— did not benefit by the Masses offered up. Religious have no right to dispose of their goods. It is contrary to holy poverty.

If you say your prayers well, the souls confided to your care will be benefited by them. God never refuses graces which are asked of Him during prayers well said.

The Purgatory of religious is much longer and more rigorous than that of people in the world, because religious abuse special graces. Many nuns are abandoned in Purgatory, by their own fault, of course, for nobody ever remembers them. Our deceased Reverend Mother has told me that God would be very pleased were the community to have a Mass said for them from time to time. Be sure and tell this to Mother Superior. God loves Reverend Mother very much. He gives her a heavy cross to prove His love for her.

No one can have a real understanding of the sufferings in Purgatory. No one thinks of them in the world. Even religious communities forget that they should pray for the poor souls and that they should inspire their pupils with this devotion. They in turn would bring this devotion to other people of the world.

Have no fear of fatigue when it is a question of serving God. Sacrifice everything for Him.

Obey your Superior promptly. Let her turn and twist you as she wills. Be very humble. Abase yourself always even, if possible, down to the earth.

M— is in Purgatory because by her underhanded remarks she often nullified the good that the Superioress could have done.

Make it a practice to live in the presence of God with a pure intention. God seeks devoted souls who will love Him for His own sake. These are very few. He wants you to be one of His true friends. Many think they love God, but they love Him for their own sakes.

We do not see God in Purgatory. That would make it Heaven. When a soul seeks God, and out of pure love desires nothing else, He never lets that soul be deceived.

God often showers graces even where malice abounds. Why should you refuse them? Devote yourself to God. Sacrifice and immolate yourself for Him. You can never do enough for Him. It is only the overflow of our piety that we can pour out on others. Put aside all human respect, even with regard to older Sisters. Always say what is necessary if it be a case of upholding the Mother Superior. It is not His great friends that God uses to annoy and cause trouble and pain to others. Thank Him that you have not been doing this. It is better to be the anvil than the hammer. You must not grow lax in the matter of denying your body and soul, for as yet you have made but little reparation for your past. The contest for your crown is hardly begun.

June (1874). Note well, that whenever a storm rages against a soul, it quietly dies down again. The devil has his agents everywhere, even in convents.

No, I do not see God when He is exposed (in the Holy Eucharist), yet I am conscious of His presence like you are with the eyes of faith. Our faith, however, is very different from yours. We know what God is. Always walk in the presence of God. Tell Him everything. Talk to Him as you would talk to a friend. Guard your interior life carefully.

In order to prepare well for Holy Communion, you must love God not only before and after receiving Him but always and at all times. God desires you to think only of Him. Mortify your mind, your eyes, your tongue; that will be far more agreeable to God than corporal penances. These (corporal penances) all too often proceed from one's own will. You must treat God as your Father, as a dear friend, as a beloved spouse. You must pour out all the tenderness of your heart on

Jesus alone and on Him wholly and entirely. During all eternity you will sing of His infinite mercy in your regard. You must love Jesus so much that He may be able to find in your heart an agreeable resting place, where He may be able, as it were, to console Himself for the many offences He receives everywhere. You must love Him for indifferent and cowardly souls but above all for yourself. In one word, you must love Him so much at V— that you will be a shining example. It is true that St. Theresa and M. Eust loved Him very much, but you have caused Him pain in the past, and you should love Him very much more in comparison to these innocent souls.

December 12, 1874. If you truly love God well He will refuse you nothing. He will give you whatever you ask.

God wishes you to concern yourself with Him alone, with His love and with the accomplishment of His holy will. When we are concerned with God, we must also of necessity think of souls. There would be but little merit in being saved alone. God expects a higher degree of perfection from you than He expects from many others.

February 1875. Watch carefully over your interior life. Keep all your small troubles for Jesus alone. He is well able to make up to you for whatever He takes from you. Your life must be one of unceasing interior acts of love and of mortification, but God alone must know of it. Do nothing extraordinary. Lead a very hidden life, yet one closely united to Jesus. Jesus wants you to love Him alone. If you put no obstacle in the way, He has extraordinary graces to bestow upon you, such as He has never yet given to anyone. He loves you in a special manner. Have you not yet noticed this? It is for us to adore His designs without seeking to fathom them. He is the Master, to do for souls whatever He wishes. Be always very humble. Lead a hidden life. Do not busy yourself with anyone. Attend to your own sanctification and affairs.

You must not have too much conversation with N—. She is too demonstrative and talkative. God does not want that of you.

It is not right of you to be thus distrustful of your Jesus. You have given Him all. Be quite convinced that He has permitted all that has happened.

Love God very much. How happy are the souls that do this. They possess a treasure! The great penance of your life will be, not the absence of your Jesus but great sorrow for all the pain you have given Him, by your failure to love Him as you desire, in return for the overwhelming number of graces which He has showered upon you and which He will continue to shower upon you.

You may rise at 4:00 A.M. and go to bed at the same time as everyone else unless you are very ill. I assure you, you will be none the worse for this. Half an hour makes but little difference and it gives edification.

Do not complain about trifles, not even to the Superioress. Keep your little sufferings to yourself and tell Jesus, to whom you ought to tell everything.

Do not be too preoccupied about your health. God will always give you sufficient strength to serve Him properly.

May 14, 1875. During your retreat, make up your mind to lose none of the graces which God will give you. Always be mindful of these graces, with a great spirit of faith and recollection. I have been telling you this for a long time. Try to be as recollected in your actions as you are during your thanksgiving after Holy Communion. Thank God for all the graces He has given you and for all those He gives you each day. Keep this in mind every morning at the end of your meditation. Also, pray for the intention I reminded you of yesterday . . . Never do anything without first recollecting yourself for a moment and seeking advice from Jesus who is in your heart . . . Yes, I love God very much, but as a soul becomes purified her love increases. Often think of the love Jesus has for you and be faithful to every inspiration of grace. Start each day as if you had as yet done nothing, but take care that you do not discourage yourself.

May 18, 1875. How small is the number of fervent religious who really have the spirit of their vocation — about one in fifty! You must at all costs be among the privileged ones. How great is the responsibility of a Superior, a Mistress of novices, a teacher! What an account they will have to render to God!

Little by little as I am being delivered, you will hear me more distinctly. When I am completely liberated, I will be a second Guardian Angel to you, but an angel that you can see.

Mother N— is still in Purgatory, because she introduced several things into the community that were not in accord with our vocation, but which tended rather to relaxation. It is a great science to be able to discern spirits. If more care were taken in receiving candidates to the religious life, there would be less trouble in communities.

June 20, 1875. God does not ask so much for strength. He would rather dwell more in our hearts. In order to obtain graces for yourself or for the community, you must renounce yourself from morning to night, seek self in nothing, let everything be hidden from the eyes of creatures. Let God alone know all your little daily sacrifices — Him alone; do you understand?

It is God who allows you to feel such distaste for many things, so that you may have more merit. Be careful to waste or lose nothing. Yes, it is true in one sense, that Jesus is more glorified when He is honored by one who was not always His friend. You are disturbed at sensing that God has chosen you to work out His designs despite your spiritual infirmities, for thus you must sacrifice and immolate yourself in return.

Do you know why God does not now grant you the graces you are asking of Him? It is because you have not enough confidence in Him. Likewise you forget the many and great graces that Jesus has given you. He pursues you from morning to night, and you avoid Him as much as you can. It is not proper for you to treat God thus, especially after He has been so kind to you. Try at every moment to look into yourself to see if you are pleasing God, examine yourself to learn if any of your acts cause Him pain. Such a constant disposition will put you more and more in favor with God. You must love God so much, that in a short time, He may truly find in your heart a welcome place to make His abode. Jesus must be able to tell you all His sorrows, such as those the world inflicts upon Him daily, and on your part, you must give Him the tender love that will console Him.

August 14, 1875. God does not want you to listen to self-love, you must trust in Him alone. I have told you this many times. Despite your faults, He can give you the necessary help to serve Him. Why do you distrust His power and goodness?

August 15, 1875. Yes, we have seen the Blessed Virgin, she has gone back to Heaven with many souls, but I am still here. You feel the heat? Alas! if you knew what the heat of Purgatory is compared to yours! A little prayer does us so much good. It is like a glass of water given to a thirsty person.

Love everyone, but do not put your trust entirely in anyone, because Jesus wants to be your great confidant. Everything for Him and for Him alone. Perform all your actions in the presence of God as I have so often told you. Consult Him before all you do or say. Let your life be one of faith and love . . . Do nothing to distinguish yourself. Without offending anyone, avoid the company of those who are too unreserved and those who are uncharitable. As for yourself, be busy about your own affairs. Keep your opinions to yourself and never express them unless obliged to do so. Be preoccupied with only that one object, the main spring of your life, Jesus. Yes, Jesus from morning to night and from night till morning.

August 20, 1875 (Retreat). Alas, I suffer more than usual in punishment for abusing many graces during my life. Perform all your deeds in the presence of God, without seeking to please anyone else. He will not leave you in peace until you have reached such a state of detachment from all created things that you will give Him your entire attention. You must be a living example for the rest of your community. Each one, on seeing your life, must be able to say, "This is the Rule." More is required of you. You must be, as it were, another Jesus. That is to say, in as far as possible, you must reproduce in your conduct the life of Jesus Himself.

September 7, 1875. Great though He is, Almighty God does not hesitate to lower Himself to the soul which loves Him. He treats with such a soul even on the smallest details that concern her. How good God is to us. Are there not secrets in our souls that God alone understands and of which we can speak to Him alone?

September 8, 1875. God permits some souls to attain a remarkable degree of tenderness in their love, whereas others do not experience great emotion. All this is part of His wise designs. In the case of those who are more capable of loving Him, He has reserved a special place for Himself in their hearts, so that they pour out their love into His adorable Heart. He is indeed the Master, giving to each one what He wills. You are one of the souls whom He has especially favored.

I suffer all night while you rest. Although I experience the pains of Purgatory at all times, still when I have permission during the day to accompany you everywhere, I suffer a little less. All this is by virtue of special dispensation of God.

November 7, 1875. Ponder well what I am going to say to you. Watch most carefully over everything you do. Ask yourself each hour if God be pleased with you, because you are to become a saint quickly. Yes, that is true, but with Divine Grace, you can accomplish everything. Acknowledge with gratitude that you are utterly unworthy of all these graces, but nevertheless, go forward.

December 8, 1875. Love God intensely. Do not fear your own suffering. Trust in Him, never in yourself. Die to yourself from morning to night . . . Do not breathe or live except for Jesus Christ. God must be your only confidant. Complain to no one except to Him. Be quite hidden from the eyes of everyone else. Sometimes you will be ill, very ill, but you will appear quite well, because God wishes to be the only witness of what passes in you. You will learn that you and your loving God will understand each other very well. If you do as God wants, namely, watch carefully over yourself so as not to lose any of His graces, He will communicate Himself to you in a special manner.

You grieve God when you do not think of Him. The union between you is like that between friends. Among friends, often one is preferred to all others. One understands us better and from him we keep no secret. If that friend noticed that we paid no attention to him, did not speak to him, or even cast a glance his way to show him that he is still our special friend, he would feel intense pain. Thus it is with God as far as you are concerned. He certainly has a great love for many of His friends, but I have told you many times, that even though you are not deserving of it as are so many others, yet He loves you in a special way. For this reason your indifference causes Him all the more pain. He awaits only a return of your inner love of heart, so that He may fill it with graces. All that you do affects Him most intimately. He loves you for thinking of Him. Despite your many occupations, He must be first in your thoughts. Whenever you have to speak to people on business, you should first glance towards Him. He has a right to this. He is the Master and may act as He pleases.

December 12, 1875. You should practice perpetual adoration in your heart at all times, not only when you go to chapel. You must also accustom yourself to make frequent spiritual communions. You will derive abundant and most salutary fruits from this, provided that you dispose yourself properly.

December 30, 1875. Never ask for anything regarding your own health. Yet do not refuse what is offered you. We must not appear singular in anything.

January 1876. Whenever you have something to say to the Superior do not be in a hurry about it unless it be something that cannot be postponed. Let what you have to say wait and thus moderate and mortify yourself.

You must prepare a dwelling place for Jesus in your heart so that later, as I have told you, He may come and rest there. You must also prepare, as well as possible, for Holy Communion. Try to think about it the evening before but especially when you awake in the morning. You must not only prepare an abode for Jesus, but also invite Him to stay with you. There would be no point in preparing a beautiful room for a guest, were you not to invite him to enter. So invite Jesus often by your desires, and above all, by your love for Him. You should become so recollected that you do not lose sight of the presence of Jesus, even when otherwise most occupied. To achieve this, watch constantly over your interior life.

About the Grotto: God will help you and supply all that you lack. If you want to please Him, do nothing about it on Sunday except pray as much as you can. That is all that is required. God desires later on to make you His helper and your heart His sanctuary.

February. In Heaven God receives infinite adoration, but as it is on earth that He is offended, He wills that also on earth, proper reparation should be made to Him, by your loving Him and consoling Him for the neglect that is heaped upon Him everywhere.

Feast of the Annunciation. When God wishes a soul to be entirely His, He begins by crushing it, very much as apples are crushed in the press — to extract its passions, its self-seeking, in a word, all its defects. When that soul is sufficiently broken, He reshapes it according to His will. If it is faithful, it is soon transformed. Only then does Jesus load it with His choicest graces and inundate it with His love.

July 16th. The Holy Eucharist must be as a magnet for you, drawing you always more and more powerfully. This Sacrament must be the main object of your life.

August 28th. Have no other desire than to love God always more and more. Try to be ever more closely united to Him. Endeavor to lead each day a more interior life, a life more closely united to your Jesus. This interior union with Jesus is brought about by your sufferings of body and soul, but above all by your longing love for Him. May you indeed conform to God›s plan by this interior life. He insists on it so pleadingly. I cannot tell you now the degree of sanctity and union with Himself to which He will lead you or what graces He has in store for you. I have, of course, spoken of some of these graces. The others are unknown to me. Guard well your actions, your very presence must inspire devotion.

August 30th. The retreat, of course, will be for all in general, but God will arrange that the sermons shall be entirely for you. Pay great attention to them. This retreat must make you a saint. God has made your heart for Himself alone. Abandon yourself entirely into our

Lord›s hands. Look neither forward nor backwards. Throw yourself entirely into His divine arms, upon His Sacred Heart, and there fear nothing. Every morning say a little prayer to our Lord and adore Him in all those churches where He is most neglected. Go there in spirit and tell Him how much you love Him and want to make up to Him for the way in which He is forsaken. You will give great pleasure to Jesus if you renew this intention several times during the day. God wishes you to think always of Him, to pray and work always under His Divine Eyes. He wants you, in as far as possible, never to lose sight of Him. All this must be done quietly, without affectation. No one must ever suspect it. Let Jesus alone know what passes between you. Keep your eyes always cast down unless when it is your duty to look after things. Then do so as modestly as possible. Do not give way to human respect. Be very humble. Make God loved as much as you can. Let everything go its own way and do you go yours in the crowd, silently. If you are obliged to come forward, do it simply and refer all to God, without disturbing yourself as to whether the affair succeeds or not. When you have done all to please Him, have no other desire but that of always loving Him more and more.

Resolve at the end of your retreat to think often of what I am going to say now. God Alone, my God and my all. Every material thing passes away, and that quickly. The Tabernacle is my place of rest, the Holy Eucharist is my life, the Cross is my portion, Mary is my Mother, Heaven is my hope . . . Yes, it would please God if you took no butter on your bread in the morning.

November 30th. You must never judge or examine the conduct of your Sisters; you will not have to give an account of their lives. Neither must you use their conduct as your model. God does not ask the same perfection from all. Mortify yourself, and do not seek to find out if others are doing all you do. God does not require it of them. You will never believe all I am telling you. This morning you witnessed what God wants you to do, as He granted you the sign you asked for. Jesus wants you to deal with Him, as with an intimate friend, without any fear whatsoever. It is true that His Majesty is frightening and that you are not worthy to have such an intimate converse with your Jesus, but is He not the Master that enriches whomsoever He wills? Ask Jesus to make you rich in every virtue, as He wishes you to be, but in the meantime, shape your life in accordance with His inspirations. Enlarge your heart because what Jesus desires above all things is to see in it His love. What wonderful graces you will receive if you are faithful, graces you have never even thought of!

Christmas 1876. When you are suffering you must not go telling everyone. It does not console you. In the first place, you should tell it to Jesus, but most often it is to Him you tell it last.

I am greatly refreshed and I think the end of my exile is not far off. Oh, if you knew how I long to see God! Amidst all these supernatural events, you must be so natural that no one will notice that anything is happening. It is the same with everything else, lead a hidden life as much as possible, but without neglecting any of your duties. Let everything be perfectly simple.

God desires that He alone should know what is going on in your soul.

January 1877. Rest peacefully on the adorable Heart of your Jesus, tell Him all your sufferings as you would tell a friend. He will understand. What I have told you about the little corner of His Heart will be revealed to you only when you are far more spiritual than you are at present. Do not worry yourself over all the troubles of your class. I pray every day for you that you may not lose patience.

February 13th. Before the Blessed Sacrament. See how Jesus is left alone. At this moment, if He wished, He could have many adorers, if they only had a little more good will! But what indifference is there even amongst religious! Our Lord is very much hurt by it. At any rate, you are to love Him for those indifferent souls and Jesus will be consoled for their neglect.

May 12th. Mortify yourself corporally, but more especially spiritually. Forget yourself. Deny yourself in everything. Never look at what others are doing. God does not demand the same perfection from everyone. All are not enlightened in the same way, but you, whom Jesus Himself enlightens, look only to Him, let Him be your aim and object in everything.

Before every action, no matter how trivial, ask yourself if what you are about to do will please Him. That is all that matters as far as you are concerned. Any act of indifference or want of regard on your part wounds Him, whereas a continual remembrance of His Holy presence, a little aspiration to Him, a look, any little attention to give Him pleasure is noticed by Him. Guard your interior well that you may lose none of His graces. Take no notice of your body. Forget yourself. Place yourself in the arms of Jesus and He will never let you be found wanting, only have unlimited confidence in His goodness. If you but realized His power, you would not put limits to His ability. What can He not do for a soul He loves!

December 13th. Never seek to please anyone by your actions, but God only. It is for Him that you must do everything. Let there be no human respect, or ever growing weary . . . He will grant anything you request of Him. Yes, it is true that you are very miserable. Humble yourself and know that Jesus does not always give His graces to the most holy.

Prepare yourself with great care for Holy Communion, Confession and the Divine Office, in a word, for anything that tends to unite you more closely to Our Lord. Many others must find it more difficult than you to see Jesus always present in their heart. After all the graces He has given you, you should have no difficulty in being recollected. I have already told you that God is searching the world over for souls that love Him with childlike affection, full of tender respect, truthfully and from the heart. He finds few such souls, fewer than you would suspect. Souls belittle the Heart of God. They look upon Jesus as too difficult to approach and thus their love for Him remains cold. Their respect for Him has degenerated into a kind of indifference. I know that all souls are not capable of understanding this love which Our Lord yearns for. Jesus has made

Himself better known to you and wants you to make up for this indifference and coldness in others. Ask Him to enlarge your heart that it may be capable of greater love. By the love and respectful familiarity with which Jesus allows you to treat Him, you can make up for that which is not granted all to understand. Do this but, above all, love much. Never grow weary in your work. Begin again each day as if you had so far done nothing. This continual renouncement of one's will and comfort and one's own opinions is a long martyrdom, but it is most pleasing to God. God wants you to be something special, not as regards your exterior, but in your inner soul. He asks of you a union with Himself, so great that you never lose sight of Him, even amidst your most absorbing occupations.

Retreat in August 1878. Great sinners who were indifferent towards God, and religious who were not what they should have been are in the lowest stage of Purgatory. While they are there, the prayers offered up for them are not applied to them. Because they have ignored God during their life, He now in His turn leaves them abandoned in order that they may repair their neglectful and worthless lives. While on earth one truly cannot picture or imagine what God really is, but we (in Purgatory) know and understand Him for what He is, because our souls are freed from all the ties that fettered them and prevented them from realizing the holiness and majesty of God, and His great mercy. We are martyrs, consumed as it were by love. An irresistible force draws us towards God who is our center, but at the same time another force thrusts us back to our place of expiation.

We are in the state of being unable to satisfy our longings. Oh, what a suffering that is, but we desire it and there is no murmuring against God here. We desire only what God wants. You on earth, however, cannot possibly understand what we have to endure. I am much relieved as I am no longer in the fire. I have now only the insatiable desire to see God, a suffering cruel enough indeed, but I feel that the end of my exile is at hand and that I am soon to leave this place where I long for God with all my heart. I know it well, I feel more at ease, but I cannot tell you the day or the hour of my release. God alone knows that. It may be that I have still many years of longing for Heaven. Continue to pray; I will repay you later on, though I do pray a great deal for you now.

Oh, how great is the mercy of God in your regard! Who can understand it? Why does Jesus act thus towards you? Why does He love you more than many others? Why has He still many greater graces to bestow on you? Is it because you deserve them? No, you even deserve them less than many others, but it is His will to act thus towards you and He is the Master of His rewards. Be very grateful. Remain always in spirit at His Divine feet and let Him act as He will. Watch well over your interior. Be very exact in finding what pleases your Jesus. Have neither eyes nor heart, nor love except for Him. Always consult Him before your smallest act. Abandon yourself wholly to His good pleasure and then be at peace. All that I have told you will be accomplished. Do not put any obstacles in the way. It is Jesus who wishes it thus.

Those who are lost are lost because they willed it, because to arrive at damnation they must have refused thousands of graces and good inspirations that God gave them, hence it is their own fault.

In answer to a question:

When I am there I will tell you, but I think the great festivals of Heaven are celebrated with an increase of ecstasy, admiration, and thanksgiving, but above all, of love. To be worthy of what I am telling you now, you must have arrived at so close a union with God that nothing disturbs you, neither sufferings, joys, success, failure, good or bad repute; nothing of any of these must influence you in any way. Jesus must be Lord of all your being and you must keep the eye of your soul constantly fixed on Him to anticipate His slightest wishes. What has Jesus not done for you and what will He not do? Let your exterior be well regulated, and let your interior be even more so. Be occupied only with what concerns yourself. Keep your eyes always lowered, speak little and in a low voice, but above all converse with Jesus always. No, you do not tire Him. This is what He expects from you. Be very kind to the children. Do not be rough with them. Be ingenious in mortifying yourself and in breaking your own will. Be especially nice to those who are less agreeable to you than to others, no matter what wrong they may have done you. This means renouncing yourself and pleasing Jesus. Nothing else matters. It is on these occasions that you must silence the human will, but you must do it because Jesus wills it. Do not allow self-love to get the upper hand, but do all blindly to please Jesus alone.

Why is it that I pray for you with less fervor than I pray for others and that often I forget to recommend you?[*]

Do not trouble yourself about that. It is a punishment for me. Even if you prayed more I should not be any the more relieved. God wills it thus. If He wants you to pray more He will inspire you to do so. I repeat again, do not be worried about me. You will never see me in my sufferings. Later on, when your soul is stronger, you will see souls in Purgatory and very awful ones, but let this not frighten you. God will then give you the necessary courage and all that you need to accomplish His holy will.

Is this not a punishment?

No, certainly not, I am here for my relief and for your sanctification. If you would but pay a little more attention to what I say.

That is true but these happenings are so extraordinary that I do not know what to make of them; it is not an ordinary thing to hear you in this way.

I quite understand your difficulty and I am aware of your sufferings on this account. However, if God wishes it and it relieves me, you will have pity on me, will you not? When I am released you will see that I will do far more for you than you have ever done for me. I already pray much for you.

Where is Sister — ?

In the lowest Purgatory, where she receives no benefit from anyone's prayers. God is often displeased, if one may speak thus, when many religious come to die, because He has called these souls to Himself that they might serve Him faithfully on earth and go straight to Heaven at the moment of death, but because of their infidelity, they have to stay long in Purgatory — far longer than people in the world who have not had so many graces.

1879, Retreat in September. We see St. Michael as we see the angels. He has no body. He comes to get the souls that have finished their purification. It is he who conducts them to Heaven. He is among the Seraphim as Monsignor said. He is the highest angel in Heaven. Our own Guardian Angels come to see us but St. Michael is far more beautiful than they are. As to the Blessed Virgin, we see her in the body. She comes to Purgatory on her feasts and she goes back to Heaven with many souls. While she is with us we do not suffer. St. Michael accompanies her. When he comes alone, we suffer as usual. When I spoke to you of the great and the second Purgatory, it was to try to make you understand that there are different stages in Purgatory. Thus I call that stage of Purgatory great or worst where the most guilty souls are, and where I stayed for two years without being able to give a sign of the torments I was suffering. The year when you heard me groaning, when I began to speak to you, I was still in the same place.

In the second Purgatory, which is still Purgatory but very different from the first, one suffers a great deal, but less than in the great place of expiation. Then there is a third stage, which is the Purgatory of desire, where there is no fire. The souls who did not desire Heaven ardently enough, who did not love God sufficiently are there. It is there that I am at this moment. Further, in these three parts of Purgatory, there are many degrees of variation. Little by little, as the soul becomes purified, her sufferings are changed.

Now are you really going to begin to rouse yourself and give yourself to God? How long have I tormented you on this subject! The retreat has been a good one and will bear fruit. The devil is not pleased.

God greatly loves the Father who gave the retreat. Tell him I thank him very much for the mementoes he promised to make for me at Holy Mass. On my part I will not be ungrateful and I will ask God to give him the graces of which he stands in need. You did well to tell him this evening all I have told you. The community has profited by his coming, but it was for you especially that he was sent. St. Michael, who has loved and protected you for so long a time, wishes that one of his missionary priests should know all that I have told you. God has His own designs in all this and you will know them later. Later on you may be able to give him more precise information about St. Michael.

You ask me if Father — is pleasing to God? This is what you are to say to him. If he continues to act as he has done up to this time, he is agreeable in God's sight. What He loves most in him is his great purity of intention, his interior spirit and his goodness to souls. Tell him if he continues to unite himself more and more to the Heart of Jesus, the closer this union becomes, the more meritorious all his actions and his entire life will be for eternity and the more profitable for souls. God does not expect ordinary perfection from him.

Tell him to be sure in his retreats and missions to recommend strongly the offering up to God of the actions of the day. This advice is not only to people in the world but also for religious communities. People do not always think enough of this and consequently many actions good in themselves will receive no reward at the last day, because they were not first offered up to God. If the Father sees that his words do not always bear the fruit he would like, let him never lose courage. He should remember that God is pleased and satisfied with his efforts even if he has succeeded in putting into the hearts of his hearers only a little love, and that only for a quarter of an hour. God has made all this known to me because the Father did not receive you badly the other day when you went to speak to him. Do all that he tells you and write down for him all that you have learned from me. Don't forget anything and profit by the advice he gives you on this subject. I tell you again that it is God who has sent him. God has great designs in your regard in all that He does in this matter. Be very faithful to all the graces that Jesus gives you. Later on, if as I hope, God makes known anything more for Father, I will tell you. Thank him again for his prayers and tell him I am not ungrateful. I will pray for him as I do for you at present.

Weigh well the idea that God wishes you to be a saint. You may say that this is nothing new because Jesus has pursued you for so long a time, and so have I, but now it is really time to begin to apply yourself seriously to this work. You saw this in a forceful manner during this retreat. Do not put any obstacles in the way of grace. Let God lead you as He wills, but above all, do not resist a single one of His inspirations. Put nature and self aside, then when you are rid of that burden, go forward without growing weary.

Pray well for me that I may soon be united to the object of my long-delayed and ardent desires. I shall be more useful to you in Heaven than I am here. That was a good thought of yours on the day the retreat closed, to invite me to come and adore Jesus present in your heart during your thanksgiving after Holy Communion. If you had done that sooner, I should have obtained much relief. Do so in the future and before all your prayers. Also offer a part of your work for me, as I have such an ardent longing to see God.

Your little note books please God very much. It is the shortest way to great perfection and close union with Jesus. I have waited long for you to show a little more love in all your actions. The more a soul loves Jesus the more meritorious all its actions are in His sight. It is only love that will be rewarded in Heaven. All that is done for any other motive will count as nothing. Love Jesus truly, once and for all, as He wants you to. Then I also shall benefit in that I shall have great relief in all my sufferings.

Is God not more pleased with me these last few days?

Yes, He is pleased because you are striving more to give Him pleasure. Have you noticed His goodness and special watchfulness over you? Has He not also given you much joy these days? He will always act like that towards you. The more you do for Him the more He will do for you. I am so happy to see that you are really beginning to love God, who is so good, and to work seriously at your perfection. If by remaining a little longer in Purgatory I could obtain that you should arrive at the perfection God demands of you in order to accomplish His designs, I would willingly bear that suffering. Never look back to examine your conduct in the past. Leave it entirely in the hands of God and go steadily forward. Your life must be summed up in two words: Love and Sacrifice. Sacrifice from morning to night, but always with Love. If only you knew what God is, there is no sacrifice that you would not be willing to make, no suffering that you would not endure for Him. If you could see Him for but one minute you would be perfectly satisfied and consoled . . . What then must it be to see Him for all eternity?

There is no middle course for you. Some souls might save themselves in other ways, but not you. You will either be a great saint or a great sinner. The choice is yours. Do you remember how a long time ago during one of your first retreats, you were much impressed by these words: *There are some souls for whom there is no middle way, they will either be angels or devils?* Apply that to yourself. You know that these words are meant for you.

August 13th. I have many things to say to you that only you and the Father will understand. Have you thought of thanking God for having sent him to you? Pray for him every day.

What is the best way of honoring St. Michael?

The best and most efficacious way of glorifying him in Heaven and honoring him on earth is to spread devotion to the souls in Purgatory, and to make known the great mission he fulfills towards these suffering souls. It is he who is entrusted by God to lead the souls to the place of expiation and to bring them to their eternal home after purification. Each time a soul arrives to increase the number of the elect, God is glorified, and this glory in some way communicates itself also to the celestial minister. It is an honor for him to present to Our Lord the souls that will sing their thanks and His mercies through all eternity. I could never make you understand the intense love which the Heavenly Archangel has for his Divine Master, and the love which God in His turn has for St. Michael. Neither can I convey to you a true idea of the love and pity St. Michael has for us. He encourages us in our sufferings by speaking to us of Heaven.

Tell the Father that if he wishes to please St. Michael, he will most earnestly recommend devotion to the souls in Purgatory. People in the world do not think of it. When they have lost their relatives or friends, they say a few prayers, weep for a few days and that is the end of it. The souls are henceforth abandoned. It is true that they merit this, for while they were on earth they neglected the dead. The Divine Judge deals with us in this world according to our actions in the former. Those who have forgotten the holy souls are forgotten in their turn. This is only fair. Perhaps if they had been reminded to pray for the dead and had been told a little about Purgatory, they might have acted differently. When God allows it, we can communicate directly with St. Michael in the way that spirits communicate.

How do they celebrate the feast of St. Michael in Purgatory?

On that day St. Michael comes to Purgatory and returns to Heaven with a great number of souls, especially with those who had been devout to him in life.

What glory does St. Michael receive from his feast day on earth?

When the feast of a saint is celebrated on earth, he receives an increase of accidental glory in Heaven, even if he is not actually remembered on earth. He receives a special recompense in memory of some particular act of heroic virtue, or of some increase of glory, which he procured for God at a given time. This reward consists in an increase of accidental glory joined to the happiness which the memory of his work on earth causes him. The accidental glory which the Archangel receives is far above that of the other saints, because this glory is proportioned to the greatness of the merit of the recipient and also to the value of the action which merits the reward.

Do you know what happens on earth?

I only know what happens in so far as God wills it. My knowledge is very limited. I have known a little about the community, but that is all. I know nothing about what goes on in the souls of other people, except in your case. That is because God allows this for your perfection. What I have sometimes told you about certain persons and what I will tell you, I only know from God at the moment. For example, I do not know what is God's will in regard to your Father's parents. Perhaps later on I may know. I will pray to God for them and recommend them to St. Michael.

I can tell you about the different degrees of Purgatory because I have passed through them. In the great Purgatory there are several stages. In the lowest and most painful, like a temporary hell, are the sinners who have committed terrible crimes during life and whose death surprised them in that state. It was almost a miracle that they were saved, and often by the prayers of holy parents or other pious persons. Sometimes they did not even have time to confess their sins and the world thought them lost, but God, whose mercy is infinite, gave them at the moment of death the contrition necessary for their salvation on account of one or more good actions which they performed during life. For such souls, Purgatory is terrible. It is a real hell with this difference, that in hell they curse God, whereas we bless Him and thank Him for having saved us.

Next to these come the souls, who though they did not commit great crimes like the others, were indifferent to God. They did not fulfill their Easter duties and were also converted at the point of death. Perhaps they were unable to receive Holy Communion. They are in Purgatory for the long years of indifference. They suffer unheard of pains and are abandoned either without prayers or if they are said for them, they are not allowed to profit by them. There are in this stage of Purgatory religious of both sexes, who were tepid, neglectful of their duties, indifferent towards Jesus, also priests who did not exercise their sacred ministry with the reverence due to the Sovereign Majesty and who did not instill the love of God sufficiently into the souls confided to their care. I was in this stage of Purgatory.

In the second Purgatory are the souls of those who died with venial sins not fully expiated before death, or with mortal sins that have been forgiven but for which they have not made entire satisfaction to the Divine Justice. In this part of Purgatory, there are also different degrees according to the merits of each soul. Thus the Purgatory of the consecrated souls or of those who have received more abundant graces, is longer and far more painful than that of ordinary people of the world.

Lastly, there is the Purgatory of desire which is called the *Threshold*. Very few escape this. To avoid it altogether, one must ardently desire Heaven and the vision of God. That is rare, rarer than people think, because even pious people are afraid of God and have not, therefore, a sufficiently strong desire of going to Heaven. This Purgatory has its very painful martyrdom like the others. The deprivation of the sight of our loving Jesus adds to the intense suffering.

Do you know each other in Purgatory?

Yes, in the manner in which souls know. There are no names in the other world. You cannot compare Purgatory and Earth. When the soul is free and released from its mortal shell, its name is buried in the grave with the body. I can only give you a small insight into the nature of Purgatory. By the light which God gives you, you are better able to understand it than others. But what is all that to the reality? Here we are lost in the will of God, whereas on earth, no matter how great the saint is, self-will always has a certain hold on him. As for us . . . we now have no more self-will at all, we know and realize only that which it pleases God to let us know, nothing more.

Do you speak to each other in Purgatory?

Souls communicate with each other when God permits it, and after the manner of souls, but without words. Yes, it is true I speak to you, but are you a spirit? Would you understand me if I did not pronounce words? But for myself, as God wills it so, I understand you without your pronouncing any words with your lips. There is communication between spirits and souls on earth. Thus when you have a good thought or a holy desire, they have been communicated to you by your Guardian Angel or by some saint, and sometimes by God Himself. That is the language of souls.

Where is Purgatory situated?

It is in the center of the earth, close to Hell, as you saw one day after Holy Communion. The large number of souls there are confined to a limited space. There are thousands and thousands of souls there. But then what space does a soul occupy? Each day thousands of souls come to Purgatory and most of them remain thirty to forty years, some for longer periods, others for shorter. I tell you this in terms of earthly calculations because here it is quite different. Oh, if people only knew and understood what Purgatory is and what it means to know that we are here through our own fault. I have been here eight years and it seems to me like ten thousand. Oh my God! Tell all this to the Father, so that he may learn from me what this place of suffering is like and may make it better known in the future. He will be able to find out for himself how profitable it is to have a great devotion to the holy souls in Purgatory. God often accords more graces through the intercession of these suffering souls than through the prayers of the saints. Let the Father, when he wishes to be sure of obtaining what he wants, ask the souls who have loved Our Lady most. These, in consequence, she wishes most of all to release. He will see whether his prayer is heard or not.

There are some souls who do not live continually in Purgatory itself . . . For instance, I accompany you wherever you go, but while you rest during the night, I suffer more, because then I am actually in Purgatory.

The Father was very right when he told you never to seek anything but the holy will of God in all you do. To see His will in all that happens to you, whether in sorrow or in joy, will be for your happiness. Oh, be doubly good in order to give pleasure to God who is so good, who is so particularly good to you. Have the eyes of your soul always open to anticipate His least wishes. Be beforehand with Him, as it were, to give Him pleasure. The more you try to please Him, the more He will give you. He will never allow Himself to be outdone in generosity. On the contrary, He always gives more than is given Him. Be unrelenting, therefore, in devoting yourself to His love and glory.

The English woman, who was drowned at Mont Michel, went straight to Heaven. She had the necessary contrition at the moment of death and at the same time the baptism of desire. All this happened through the intervention of St. Michael. What a happy shipwreck!

About Father P— who is retired, St. Michael is not pleased about that. But God leaves one free. He wishes to have in His service only those who serve Him willingly without ever looking back. Tell Father P— God wants him to continue with great courage to accomplish all that he has undertaken for His sake. Tell him to be prudent and not undertake more than his strength will allow. I am praying for all his intentions, and as I told you before, I pray for him as I do for you.

Pius IX went straight to Heaven. He had his Purgatory on earth.

How do you know M. P. — went straight to Heaven as you did not see her pass through Purgatory?

God made this known to me. It is through His goodness that I know the things you ask me, when I have not seen or experienced them myself.

The justice of God keeps us in Purgatory, and we deserve it, but His mercy and His fatherly Heart does not leave us here bereft of all consolation. We ardently desire complete union with Jesus, but He desires it almost as much as we do. On earth, He sometimes communicates Himself to certain souls in a most intimate manner (to few, because, so few will listen to Him) and He delights in revealing His secrets to them. The souls that receive these favors are those that seek to please Him in all their conduct and who live and breathe only for Jesus and try to please Him.

There are in Purgatory very culpable souls but they are repentant, and notwithstanding the sins they have to expiate, they are confirmed in grace and can no longer sin. They are perfected as the soul is purified by degrees in this place of expiation. The soul understands God better, without, however, the soul seeing God, because then there would no longer be any Purgatory. If in Purgatory, we did not know God better than He is known on earth, our suffering would not be so keen and our martyrdom so cruel. Our main torment is the absence of Him who is the sole object of our long-endured desires.

The three friends of V. P. — have been in Heaven for a long time.

Then what happened to the prayers Father P— said for them?

Those in Heaven for whom prayers are said on earth can apply those prayers to the souls they wish to benefit. It is a very consoling thought for those in the other world to know that their relatives and friends on earth do not forget them, even though they have no further need of prayers. In return, they are not ungrateful.

The judgments of God are very different from those of the world. He takes into account the temperament and character of each and what is done by carelessness or pure malice. To Him who knows the most secret recesses of the heart, it is not difficult to see what goes on there. Jesus is very good, but He is also most just.

What is the distance between Purgatory and the earth we inhabit?

Purgatory is in the center of the globe.

Is not the earth itself a Purgatory?

Amongst the people who dwell there some, by voluntary or accepted penance, do their Purgatory on earth because it is truly a place of suffering, but these souls, not having sufficient generosity, go to the real Purgatory to finish what was begun on earth.

Are sudden and unprepared deaths acts of God's justice or of His mercy?

Such deaths are sometimes an act of justice, sometimes one of mercy. When a soul is timid and God knows it is well prepared to appear before Him, He takes it out of this world suddenly to spare it the terrors it might experience at the last moment. Sometimes, also, God takes souls in His justice. They are not for this reason eternally lost, but their Purgatory is much more severe and prolonged than it would otherwise have been, since they were either deprived of the Last Sacraments or received them hastily and so were unprepared for their passage into eternity. Others having filled up the measure of their crimes and having remained deaf to all inspirations of Divine Grace are taken by God out of this world so that they may not excite His vengeance still more.

Is the fire of Purgatory like that of earth?

Yes, with this difference, that the fire of Purgatory is a purification prescribed by God's justice and that of earth is very mild compared to that of Purgatory. It is a shadow compared to the furnace of Divine Justice.

How can a soul burn?

By a just and express permission of God, the soul which is the real culprit (for the body only obeys the soul) suffers as if the body were suffering. Have you ever seen any evil committed by a dead body?

Tell me what happens during the agony and after. Does the soul find itself in light or darkness? Under what form is the sentence pronounced?

I had no agony as you know, but I can tell you this, that at the last decisive moment, the devil lets loose all his rage against the one that is dying. God permits souls to go through these last trials in order to increase their merits. Souls that are strong and generous, in order that they may have a more glorious place in Heaven, have often had, at the end of their lives and in the moment of death, terrible combats with the angel of darkness. You have been witness to this. But they always come out victorious. God never allows a soul that has been devoted to Him during life to perish at the last moment. Those souls who have loved the Blessed Virgin and invoked her all their lives receive from her many graces in their last struggles. It is the same for those who have been really devout to St. Joseph, to St. Michael, or to any of the saints. I have already said one is glad to have an intercessor with God in those dreadful moments. Some souls die quite tranquilly without experiencing any of those trials. God has His designs in everything. He does or permits all for the good of each particular soul.

How can I describe what happens after the agony? It is impossible really to understand it unless one has passed through it. When the soul leaves the body it is as if it were lost in or, if I may say so, surrounded by God. It finds itself in such a bewildering light that in the twinkling of an eye it sees its whole life spread out, and at this sight, it sees what it deserves, and this same light pronounces its sentence. The soul does not see God but is annihilated in His presence. If the soul is guilty as I was and, therefore, deserves to go to Purgatory, it is so crushed by the weight of the faults that still remain to be blotted out, that it hurls itself into Purgatory. It is only then that one understands God and His love for souls and what a terrible evil sin is in the eyes of the Divine Majesty. St. Michael is present when the soul leaves the body. I saw him only, and he is the only one that every soul sees. (Later) I also saw my Guardian Angel. From this you can understand why it is said, "St. Michael conducts souls to Purgatory", for a soul is not taken, but he is there at the carrying out of each sentence. All that happens in this other world is a mystery for yours.

What happens when a soul goes straight to Heaven?

For that soul, its union with Jesus continues after death. That is Heaven, but the union in Heaven is much closer and more intimate than that of earth.

Why did you behave so badly towards God today? He is not pleased with your conduct and He is so good to you. It is real ingratitude on your part. Why do you bother about the conduct of others? Busy yourself with your own, that is enough. Everybody has not the same disposition, and if you were to have "lost your head" on account of all the frights I have given you these seven years past you would have lost it long ago. It will be a long time before that takes place. Set your mind at rest, therefore, and do not begin to act as you did today.

You have good reason not to like ecstasies. They must of necessity be accepted when God sends them, but He does not wish that anyone should desire them. Those are not the sort of things that lead one to Heaven. A humble and mortified life is much more to be desired and is much safer. It is true that many of the saints had revelations and ecstasies but they were a reward which God gave them after long combats and a life of self-abnegation, or else, because He wished to use those servants of His for great things to procure His glory. That was done without any notice or fuss, in silence and prayer, and if they became known, the souls were covered with confusion and only spoke of their experiences under obedience.

Almighty God has crushed you in the past, but you must be very patient and take courage, because He will annihilate you still more in the future.

Tell Mother Superior that if she meets persons of the temperament and character of Sister — to take no notice of them, and never listen to all they want to say to her.

Be quite easy as to what you told me. This is how you know if a grace is truly given by God. These graces come unexpectedly and fall on you like a gentle shower of rain, that takes you by surprise when the sky appears cloudless. There is no danger in this case to fear having sought them, as you were not even thinking of such things. You have noticed this many times. It is quite different with graces that one thinks are given by Jesus, but are the effect of the imagination, which has worked hard to produce them. These should be feared because the devil often plays his part in them and takes advantage of a weak brain or a soft temperament, or a judgment not too sane. He then deceives the poor souls, who in reality do not sin, provided they follow the advice of those who guide them spiritually. I can tell you there are many in the world of this type. The devil acts in this way to make religion look ridiculous. Such souls seek themselves while they think they seek God and dream of a sanctity that is false.

Tell me, in what does true sanctity consist?

You know that very well, but as you wish it I shall repeat it to you, though I have already told it to you many times. True sanctity consists in renouncing oneself from morning to night, in being a living sacrifice, in constantly putting aside the human self, in allowing God to work in and with you as He pleases, to receive the graces He sends you with profound humility, recognizing yourself quite unworthy of them, to live as constantly as possible in the Divine Presence, to perform all your actions under the eye of God, wanting Him only to be the witness of your efforts and your only reward. This is the sanctity wished for and demanded by Jesus of all those who desire to be His only and to live His life. All the rest is pure illusion.

Some souls have their Purgatory on earth by suffering, others by love, for love is a true martyrdom. The soul that really tries to love Jesus finds that notwithstanding all its efforts it does not love Him as much as it wants to, and that is for that soul a perpetual martyrdom caused by a love which is not without great suffering. It is, as I told you, rather like the state of a soul in Purgatory, who continually leaps up towards Him who is its only desire, and who at the same time is hurled back because its expiation is not completed.

Ask Reverend Mother sometimes to allow you to read over what I tell you instead of your ordinary spiritual reading. Take one day a week, Thursday for instance, because what is the good of writing it down if you never read it over. You end by forgetting it, and it is not for that reason I tell it to you, but in order that you may profit by it.

If I had never spoken to anyone of what you have told me, what would be the result? You know I had a strong inclination to keep it entirely to myself.

You were quite at liberty to keep it all to yourself, but in that case, I should have advised you to speak, because God has never permitted that the perfecting of any soul should come directly from Heaven.

Since people live on earth, God wills that they work out their sanctification by the advice which He permits them to receive for this end. You did well to speak when it cost you so much to do so. Anyway there is nothing of all this your own, and God who directs all events for the good of those He loves, knows how to draw glory for Himself at the same time.

November 1879. The sister-in-law of N— is in Purgatory where she is suffering much. The Reverend Father can help her by offering the holy sacrifice of the Mass for her.

The old sinner was saved through the mercy of God like so many others. He is in the great Purgatory.

Does All Souls' Day and its octave bring great joy to Purgatory and many releases?

On All Souls' Day many souls leave the place of expiation and go to Heaven. Also, by a special grace of God on that day only, all the suffering souls, without exception, have a share in the public prayers of the Church, even those who are in the great Purgatory. Still the relief of each soul is in proportion to its merits. Some receive more, some less, but all feel the benefit of this extraordinary grace. Many of the suffering souls receive this one help only in all the long years they pass here and this by the justice of God. It is not, however, on All Souls' Day that the most go to Heaven. It is on Christmas night.

There are many things that I could tell you but I am not allowed to do so. It is you who must ask me, then I may answer.

I am very much relieved by the prayers of good Father P—. Tell him I thank him very much for them, as also for those he has had the charity to get said for me. I always pray for him, as I told you, and I hope to do so still more when I am in Heaven. Tell him, also, I know when he prays for me, and it is the same with the other souls in Purgatory . . . Very few souls get any prayers, the majority are totally abandoned and no thought or prayers are given them on earth.

About the time of our release we know nothing. If we only knew when the end of our sufferings would come it would be an intense relief, a joy for us, but no, it is not so. We know well that our sufferings decrease and our union with God becomes closer, but what day (that is according to earthly calculations, because here there are no days) we shall be united to God, of that we know nothing; it is a secret. The souls in Purgatory have no knowledge of the future except what God sometimes gives them. According to their merits, some souls have more of this knowledge than others, yet what do all these things matter to us, unless it is a question of the glory of God or of the good of souls? You need not be astonished that the devil or his agents sometimes foretell future events that really come to pass. The devil is a spirit and, in consequence, has many more wiles and ways of finding out things than any person on earth, except the few saints whom God enlightens in a special manner. He roams about everywhere trying to do harm. He sees what is going on all over the world and with his extraordinary sagacity foresees many things before they happen. That is the only explanation. Woe to those who make themselves his slaves by consulting him. This is a sin very displeasing to God.

Can the souls ever be mistaken? Would God allow this?

Yes, not about existing things but about the future. Yet there is no imperfection on their part in all this. Does not God Himself sometimes seem to change the order of His plans?* For example, it may happen that God wishes to chastise a kingdom, a province, or person.

---

* This way of speaking is adapted to human language which only takes notice in time of the succession of events and changes. But there is no time with God, therefore, no succession and no change. His decrees foreseen and decided on from all eternity are unchangeable and eternal as He is Himself.

That is the intention He seems to manifest. But by prayers or other means taken by that country, province or person to disarm God's anger, He may grant full forgiveness or a partial remission of His designs according to His infinite wisdom. Often He also allows events to be foretold, or He gives knowledge of them to some soul so that they may warn others and appease His vengeance. His mercy is so great that He only punishes in the very last extremity.

In the case of the person of whom you spoke to me the other day, I did not at that moment tell you the events as they turned out. However, it was thus that God made me see them, but because she changed her conduct somewhat, God only gave her half the punishment which He had in store for her if she had continued in her former dispositions. In this way we can often appear to be mistaken.

Are many Protestants saved?

By the mercy of God a certain number of Protestants are saved, but their Purgatory is for many long and rigorous. It is true they have not abused grace like many Catholics, but neither have they had the marvelous graces of the sacraments and the other helps of the true religion, thus their expiation in Purgatory is prolonged.

I am speaking lower than usual, because for the last eight days you have been speaking in too low a voice to God in saying the Divine Office. When you begin to speak louder, I will do the same.

Do you know in Purgatory about the persecution of the Church? Do you know when it will end?

We know that the Church is being persecuted and we pray for her triumph, but when this will be, I do not know. Some of the souls may know, but I do not. In Purgatory the souls are not entirely occupied by their sufferings. They pray for all the interests of God and for those who shorten their sufferings. They pray and thank God for His infinite mercies in their regard, because the space between Purgatory and Hell for some of them was very narrow and they barely escaped falling into Hell. Judge then what the gratitude of those souls is who were barely rescued from Satan.

I cannot explain to you how it is that we no longer see the earth as you do. This can only be understood when the soul has left the body, because then the earth which it has left, leaving there its body, seems to it as a mere speck compared with the vast unending horizons of eternity which then open before it.

You must never take any notice of what will be said of you. The real merit of a person consists not in accepting with patience rebukes which she has merited more or less, but in accepting patiently those she has not merited, especially if she has done her utmost to do good and is then reproached for it.

I receive far more relief from one of your actions done in union with Jesus, than from a vocal prayer, because what is it that God hears? He hears all that is done with an interior spirit. The more closely a soul is united with God the more readily does He grant all it asks.

A soul intimately united with Jesus is the mistress of His Heart. Strive then after this union which Jesus has desired to have with you for so long. You want to please Him? Well, this is the only way. You approach closer to His Heart by great attention to the least manifestations of His holy will. He must be able to twist and turn you as He likes and He must never find any resistance on your part. When you have arrived at that point you will begin to see and understand His goodness. Be really in earnest about working for God alone. Never seek any witness but Him for any of your actions. Be very careful never to say to yourself, when performing any act no matter how trivial it may be, such as, "If I do things this way I shall please so and so. I will do this to please such a person." God does not like these human reasonings in anyone, still less in you. Direct your intentions always with the sole desire of pleasing Jesus, and Him only. If by so acting, you manage to please someone else, so much the better, and if the contrary happens, that cannot be helped. God will be pleased and that is all that ought to matter to you.

December 8th — 2:00 o'clock — The Immaculate Conception — Alas, how many lives seem to be filled with good works and at death are found empty. This is because all those actions that appeared to be good, all those showy works, all that conduct that seemed irreproachable — all these were not done for Jesus alone. Some will have their eyes opened when they come here to this life (in Purgatory). On earth they wanted to be made much of, to shine, to be thought very exact in religious observances, to be esteemed as perfect religious. This is the mainspring of so many lives. If you only knew how few people work for God and act for Him alone. Alas, at death, when they are no longer blinded, what regrets they will have. If only sometimes they would think of eternity. What is life compared to that day which will have no evening for the elect, or to that night which will have no dawning for the damned? On earth, people attach themselves to everything and everyone except to Him, who alone ought to have our love and to whom we refuse it. Jesus in the Tabernacle waits for souls to love Him and He finds none. Hardly one soul in a thousand loves Him as it should. You love Him and make up to Him for this guilty indifference which exists all over the world.

But in Purgatory souls really love, do they not?

Yes, but it is a love of reparation, and if on earth we had loved Him as we ought to have done, there would not be so many of us here in this place of expiation.

Is Jesus well-loved in Heaven?

In Heaven they love Him very much, there He is compensated. But Jesus wants more than that. He wants to be loved on earth, on that earth where He annihilates Himself in every Tabernacle, in order to be approached more easily and yet He is refused. People pass before a church with more indifference than they would before any public monument. If by chance, they go into the holy place, it is only to insult still more the Divine Captive who dwells there, namely, by their coldness and their irreverence. Their prayers are said hurriedly and without attention, instead of speaking to Him from their hearts and saying words of friendship and gratitude for all His favors to them.

Tell Father P— that God expects from him this love which He so rarely meets with. He expects it from him who comes each day so close to Jesus, whom he receives into his heart. Oh, tell him that in those blessed moments he may repair by his tender love the indifference of so many ungrateful souls. His heart must melt with love before Jesus in the Host and intercede for those priests who enjoy the same privilege that he does, yet treat the sacred mysteries with a frozen heart which remains as cold as marble to Jesus. Every day let his union with God become closer, in order to prepare himself worthily for the great graces which Jesus has in store for him.

I have told you there are some souls who do their Purgatory at the foot of the altar. They are not there for faults they have committed in church, because those faults which attack Jesus directly, Jesus present in the Tabernacle, are punished with terrible severity in Purgatory. The souls that are there in adoration are there as a reward for their reverent behavior in the Sacred Presence. They suffer less than if they were in Purgatory itself, and Jesus, whom they contemplate with the eyes of their soul and of faith, softens their pains by His invisible Presence.

January 1880. On Christmas night, thousands of souls leave their place of expiation for Heaven, but many remain, and I am of their number. You sometimes say to me that the perfecting of a soul is a long process and you are also astonished that after so many prayers, I am so long deprived of the sight of God. Alas, the perfecting of a soul does not take any less time in Purgatory than upon earth. There are a number of souls, but they are very few, who have only a few venial sins to expiate. These do not stay long in Purgatory. A few well-said prayers, a few sacrifices soon deliver them. But when there are souls like mine — and that is nearly all whose lives have been so empty and who paid little or no attention to their salvation — then their whole life has to be begun over again in this place of expiation. The soul has to perfect itself all over again, and love and desire Him, whom it did not love sufficiently on earth. This is the reason why the deliverance of some souls is delayed. God has given me a very great grace in allowing me to ask for prayers. I did not deserve it, but without this I would have remained like most of those here, for years and years more.

Do religious and those of the same family communicate together?

In Purgatory, as in Heaven, religious and those of the same family are not always together. Souls do not all merit the same punishment or the same reward. Still in Purgatory we do recognize others and if God permits it we may communicate with one another.

Are you able to receive a prayer or a thought of friends who are dead, and let them know of the remembrance we have of them?

Thoughts of earth can be made known here, but there is not much in all that, because I have already told you that the souls in Purgatory know those persons who interest themselves in their behalf on earth. God sometimes allows those on earth to receive a prayer, a warning or some information. All that I told you about St. Michael was from himself and all that I said about your Father was from God.

All the commissions that you have so often given me for the other world, I have always done, but all these things are subordinate to the Divine Will.

Does everyone in Purgatory know the faults of the others as they will be known at the last judgment?

In general we do not know about the faults of one another, except in some rare cases when God has particular designs with regard to certain souls, but it is to few that He acts in this way.

Have you a more perfect knowledge of God than we have?

What a question! Of course we know Him far better and love Him far more. Indeed, it is just that which causes our greatest suffering. On earth you simply do not know what God is. There, each one of you has an idea of what you think God is, according to your very limited knowledge, but when we leave our covering of clay and when nothing impedes the liberty of our souls, we at last begin to know God, His goodness, His mercy, His love. After this clearer view and the thirst for union, our souls yearn for God. This is our very life and we are forever repulsed because we are not sufficiently pure. This, in a word, is our worst suffering, the hardest, the most bitter. Oh, if only we were allowed to come back to earth, after knowing what God really is, what a different life we would lead! But what useless regrets, and yet on earth you do not think of these things and live as if you were blind. Eternity is of no account to you. The earth, which is only a journey and receives only the body which in itself turns to dust, is the sole object to which almost all of your desires tend and you do not even think of Heaven while Jesus and His love are entirely forgotten.

Do the souls in Purgatory console each other mutually?

In Purgatory our only consolation, our only hope is in God alone. On earth, God sometimes allows us to be consoled in our sufferings of soul or body by the heart of a friend, but then again if the love of Jesus does not fill that heart, the consolations are vain. Here the souls are lost, drowned as it were, in the Divine Will and God alone can soften their pains. Each soul is tormented according to its guilt, but all have one common sorrow that surpasses all the rest, the absence of Jesus who is our very element, our life, our all. And we are separated from Him through our own fault.

After an action you must not waste your time going over it to examine if you have done well or ill. Certainly you must examine your actions each day to be able to do better in the future, but this must not be at the expense of the soul.

God loves simple souls. You must go to Him, therefore, with good will, always ready to sacrifice yourself to please Him. You must act with Jesus as a little child does with its mother, trusting in His goodness and placing all your spiritual and temporal interest with great confidence in His Divine Hands. Having done this, try to please Him in everything without troubling yourself about anything else. God does not regard great acts or heroic deeds as much as He does simple actions or small sacrifices, provided these are done with love for Him.

Sometimes even a tiny sacrifice, which was known only to God and to the soul, may be far more meritorious than a great one that was loudly applauded. One must be very interior in order not to take for oneself any of the praise given one. God seeks souls empty of self so as to fill them with His love. He finds but a few. Self-love leaves no place for Jesus. Do not let any opportunity to mortify self pass by, especially interior mortification. Jesus has many graces to give you during Lent. Therefore, prepare yourself by a redoubling of your fervor, but above all, love Jesus. He is so little loved by the world and so outraged by it.

The Blessed Virgin loves you very much. On your part love her with all your heart and do all you can to procure her the greatest possible glory.

You will never be able to understand well enough the goodness of God. If people only took the trouble to think about it sometimes, it would be enough to make them all saints, but they do not sufficiently know the merciful goodness of the Heart of Jesus in the world. Each one measures it according to his way of thinking and this way is wrong. This is the reason why they pray badly. Yes, very few people pray as Jesus wants them to pray. They are wanting in confidence and yet Jesus only grants our prayers according to the ardor of our desires and the strength of our love. This is why the graces we often ask for remain ineffective.

To be happy in religion we should be deaf, dumb and blind. That is to say, we must hear many things that we could repeat but which are far better kept to ourselves. We shall never be sorry for having kept silent. We are obliged to see and hear many things and to act as if we had neither seen nor understood.

Oh, if you only knew how paltry these little nothings are about which some make such a fuss. The devil makes use of these little straws to check the progress of a soul and obstruct all the good that she is called to do. Do not let yourself be caught in these meshes. Have a large heart and pass over all these little miseries without even noticing them. Jesus should be a sufficient attraction for you to prevent your being hindered by anything whatsoever outside of Him. See everything as coming from His bounty, whether He afflicts or consoles you. It is His love that arranges everything for the benefit of His friends. Never allow yourself to be discouraged. In a few hours, or even in the twinkling of an eye, Jesus could bring you to the summit of perfection which He desires for you. But no, He prefers your own efforts and He wants you to see for yourself how hard and rugged is the way to perfection.

Be very generous. Jesus has bestowed more graces on you than on many others and He will give you still more, but in return He hopes to find in you a soul devoted to Him and ready for any sacrifice.

Above all, He wants of you great love, and when you have fought against yourself and your failings and acted in a spirit of profound faith, then will faith seem a reality. Before this can take place, you must act as if Jesus were always visibly present to you in a natural way, whereas His presence is supernatural.

Preachers and directors of souls do good only in proportion to their union with Jesus. In their spirit of prayer and in watching over their interior, they must always have their eyes directed towards Jesus, sacrificing all for the salvation of the souls entrusted to their care.

Are the promises made to those who recite the rosary of St. Michael true?

The promises are real, but you need not think that people who recite it out of routine and without any pains to become holy are taken out of Purgatory at once. That would be false. St. Michael does more than he promises, but he is not over anxious to relieve those who are condemned to a long Purgatory. Certainly as a reward for their devotion to the Archangel their sufferings are shortened, but as to delivering them at once, not so. I, who used to say it, can serve as an example of this. Immediate deliverance takes place only in the case of those who have worked with courage at their perfection and who have little to expiate in Purgatory.

France is indeed very guilty, but unfortunately she is not the only one. At this moment there is not a single Christian kingdom that is not openly or by underhanded means trying to expel God from its midst. The secret societies, and their master, the devil, are fomenting and stirring up all this trouble.

This is now the hour of the prince of darkness. While he is in power he may do his worst, but God will show that He alone is Master. He may use severity to manifest His power, but even in His vengeance, Jesus is yet always merciful.

By the permission of God we in Purgatory know what is happening on earth at this moment so that we may pray for those great needs, but our prayers alone will not suffice. If Jesus could only find some really good souls who were willing to make reparation and disarm His outraged Majesty, it would indeed please His Divine Heart now deluged by so much bitterness. Such souls might obtain His mercy, since God desires to pardon those who humble themselves. Tell this to Mother Superior.

St. Michael will intervene in the personal struggle of the Church which is so terribly persecuted, but not so easily destroyed as the wicked think. It is he who is also the special patron of France and who will help her to take her rank as the eldest daughter of the Church, because, notwithstanding all the wickedness that is committed in France, there is still much good and so many devoted souls there. I do not know when St. Michael will intervene; you must pray much for this intention. Invoke the Archangel, remind him of his titles and beseech him to intercede with Christ, over whose Heart he has such influence. But be sure that the Blessed Virgin is not forgotten. France is her kingdom, privileged over all others. She will save it. Those who promote the recitation of the Rosary everywhere deserve praise. It is this prayer that is the most efficacious in the present time of need.

The heroic act is very pleasing to God and of great help to the souls in Purgatory, and very helpful to the generous souls who make it. By giving up a part of their merits, they do not lose but actually gain.

As for the plenary indulgences, I may as well tell you that few, very few people gain them entirely. There has to be such a wonderful disposition of heart and will that it is rare, much rarer than you think it is, to have the entire remission of one's faults. In Purgatory, we receive only the indulgences applied to us by way of suffrage, as God permits according to our dispositions.

It is true that we have no inclination to sin, but we are no longer in the reign of Mercy but under that of Divine Justice, so that we receive only what God wants us to have. When a soul is near the object of its desires, namely Heaven, it may be delivered and admitted to eternal joy by the efficacy of one plenary indulgence well gained, or even gained only in half and applied to its intentions, but for other souls it is not so. They have often during life despised or made little use of indulgences, and God who is always just, rewards them according to their works. They gain something, as it pleases God, but hardly ever the full benefit of the indulgence.

May 1880. Work without ceasing and with all your strength at your own perfection. If you want to, you can become what Jesus wishes you to be, for you have enough strength of character to overcome all the difficulties which stand in the way of your union with Him. Your life will be a continual martyrdom, but a martyrdom in which you will nevertheless taste the sweetest joys. When a soul suffers, He for whom she suffers gives her at each sacrifice, each renunciation, a fresh grace which encourages her to go steadily onward in her devotedness. Nothing gives Jesus greater pleasure than to see a soul that notwithstanding all the obstacles which obstruct her path, forces herself to be ever more and more devoted in procuring the glory of God and promoting His love.

You are sad in seeing how God is insulted in Paris, but those poor people do not know what they are doing, in spite of all their blasphemies. Jesus is much more outraged by the sins of those consecrated to Him than by the more violent crimes of those who are not His friends. How many souls whom Jesus has called to perfection remain always worthless because they have not corresponded to Divine Grace. One must put oneself out and constantly check and keep oneself up to a very high standard to be happy in God's service. How very few interior souls there are in the world, and even in religious communities. Each one seeks her own ease and comfort and refuses to be inconvenienced in the smallest thing. And yet God would be so happy (if one may so speak) if they would only love Him without constraint and with all their hearts. If He could only find such joy in this community, what innumerable graces He would shower upon it. For yourself, work your hardest at self-conquest and at loving Jesus, which He has been seeking from you for such a long time. Jesus desires that you should love Him with the love of a child, that is, with the tenderness with which a child seeks to give pleasure to beloved parents. You are still so cold towards Jesus and this is not what He expects of you when He in turn loves you so much.

August 1880. There are numbers of useless actions, many days entirely futile, without any love for Jesus or purity of intention. They are all lost since they have no value for Heaven.

You do not direct your intention with the purity that God wills. For instance, instead of offering up your actions vaguely, you could do so with much more fruit, if you only made your intention more definite. When you take your meals for example, say, "O my Jesus nourish my soul with your Divine Grace while I nourish my body." When you wash your face and hands say, "My Jesus, purify my soul as I am purifying my body," and so on, for each of your actions. Accustom yourself to be always speaking heart to heart with Jesus, and let Him be the mainspring of all you do or say. Do you understand me?

You must never excuse yourself. What difference does it make to you whether others think you guilty if you are innocent? And if you see that you have failed in any way, humble yourself and keep silence. Never excuse yourself even in your own thoughts.

September 2nd — Retreat. You told the Father this morning that it annoyed you very much to hear me and that you would prefer to be like everyone else. During the year you wrote the same thing to him and you have often said the same to Mother Superior. Why do you fret like this? Is it not God who allows everything? It has nothing to do with you. Try to profit by these graces and stop complaining. You have not yet heard all that you will hear and you have not yet seen all that you will see. Tell that to your Father and tell him also that I am not the devil. He does not think so. It is you only who have these fears. Calm yourself and profit by this retreat. From this moment you must change absolutely. Do not give way to all these reflections thinking only about yourself. That is self-love and nothing else. Instead open your heart to grace, cling to Jesus and do not waste your precious time in wondering why this and why that.

God plans to give you great graces, and to him also whom He has sent to you to tell you what He wants from you. Adore His designs without seeking to understand them. The Father will say many things in the sermons which are for you, though he will not think of that. Jesus allows this; therefore, profit by this holy retreat for it will be decisive for you.

It is only those actions done with great love and under the eye of God, wishing to do His Holy Will, that will receive their reward immediately, without the soul passing through Purgatory. What great blindness there is in the world about all this.

November. The retreat is finished for all the rest, but for you it must not finish at all. You must go on with it all the year and always in your heart, even in the midst of your most absorbing occupations. Have your own little cell where you can recollect yourself and speak heart to heart with Jesus and never lose sight of Him. Last year you were too much distracted. Now it must be so no longer. You have promised God and you have also promised the Father that you are going to begin a new life. You must then, keep your word at any price. It will cost you effort, but will it cost you less later on? No, alas, everything passes so quickly and you, like the rest, do not pay attention to this. Jesus has been pursuing you for such a long time, surely you will not refuse to abandon yourself entirely into His Hands after all the graces He has showered upon you? If you would only let Him have His way, you would become a saint and He wants you to be a great saint. Has the Father not told you again during these days, in the name of God, that there is no middle course for you? How many people have already told you the same thing and you are indifferent, though these warnings should have been sacred to you. It seems to me that this time you have paid more attention to and have been more impressed by this word, again repeated to you. Think often about it, for it is very serious. I have told you that Jesus is waiting for a small effort on your part and He will do the rest. Be very generous. What could you not obtain from God if only you were what

He wants you to be. What a close union He desires to have with your soul. What joys He has in store for you, if you only knew how good Jesus is to you. Often reflect upon the choice gifts bestowed on you. Mother Superior told you that it was especially for you that she asked for the same Father this year for the retreat, and you did not believe her. Nevertheless it was true. She followed the inspiration given her by God, who wished you to know the Father better and also that he should know you better. Profit by this grace, which will not be the last. Put into practice all he tells you to do. You are free, so open to him your heart so that he may read it like a book. If he only knew you as I do. One does not know you at first sight; it takes time.

All those thoughts you had yesterday were diabolical. The devil will do his utmost to hinder the good that will be done in spite of him. Cherish most gratefully all the graces of the retreat and never lose sight of them. Do not be afraid to sacrifice yourself from morning to night in order to do God's will. He will reward you magnificently.

Why was I so thrilled when I heard the Father's first words?

That was already the prelude to the graces which you were to receive during the retreat. There are certain attractions between souls which are not understood here on earth. God has made the soul of that Father and yours for each other, and that is why you were so impressed when he spoke and you will often experience the same sentiment in the future. Pray much for this Father, whom Jesus has given you to help you to raise your soul to Him. He needs stronger and higher graces than most people, in order not to be discouraged. In his work he meets with repulsive and tiring days that impose upon his nature. His life is hard and penitential. You must help him by your prayers. So far you have done so but it is not enough. You must offer up your works and some of your exterior sufferings, some of your sacrifices, in a word, unite his intentions to all you do and unite yourself with his works.

Jesus has great designs upon him as he has also upon you, for this reason He allows you to speak to him and open your heart to him. Regard him as your father and be submissive to him as a true child, and God will be pleased. Do not be disturbed because I say all this to you. You have been carrying out most of what I said to you. I had to tell you this and you must repeat it to the Father. Do you hear me?

This retreat has been very pleasing to God and very profitable to souls. It is with joy that Jesus sees the souls of religious turning to Him and seeking Him as their one end. It is for this that Jesus calls them into His service, but how easy it is on earth to forget what is most sacred.

A good retreat helps souls to renew their first fervor and this is what happened in the one you have just made. It has greatly consoled the Sacred Heart of Jesus.

What are the few moments we have to pass on earth compared to eternity? At the hour of death, you will not find that you have done too much. Be very generous, do not listen to yourself but always look at the goal to which Jesus calls you. That is sanctity, pure love. Then go forward and never look back. Great crosses, crosses that often break the heart, so to say, are the portion of God's own friends.

You recently complained to Jesus that He had sent you very many sorrows this year. It is true, but why do you find these crosses so heavy? It is because you do not love enough, and yet, you have not come to the end of your trials. Those that you have had up to now are only the forerunners of what you may expect. Did I not tell you that you would suffer always in body and in soul, and often in both together? There is no holiness without suffering. When you allow grace to work freely in you, when Jesus really reigns over your will and you allow Him to be absolute master of your whole being, then, no matter how heavy the crosses are, you will not feel their weight. Love will absorb everything, but until that time comes you will suffer, and suffer much, because the soul does not in one minute detach itself from everything so as to act only for pure love. God sees your efforts with pleasure. Oh, if only He were better known and understood on earth. But no, He is forgotten. At least, do you love Him and console Him.

Let your efforts always grow in intensity so as to give Him more pleasure. Work hard without relaxing, so that you may soon reach the degree of sanctity that He desires of you.

September 16th. You are a little more satisfied with yourself these last few days, and so is Jesus, because you are making efforts to please Him and to become more closely united to Him. But do not think that it is as yet completed. It is but a tiny beginning of the union He desires to have with your soul. Oh, how little people on earth understand what a degree of detachment Jesus demands of a soul whom He wishes to make all His own. People think they love and will soon become saints because they feel a little more sensible devotion than usual, but all these natural devotions are as nothing. A soul must rise up and detach itself from its self-love, its passions, in order to free itself from all human love. It is hard, and how few there are who understand what all this means. You who, by the great mercy of God, do understand a little of it, you whom He loves so much, begin to follow His path of self-denial and death to yourself. Think often of all the marks of His love Jesus has given to you. Consider how far He went to seek you and how He smoothed away all the obstacles in your path. He has done more for you than for anyone else. Each day He loads you with His choicest graces. Just reflect how generous He has been to you these last days. In return, He expects great generosity on your part, more than from others whom He has not blessed so richly and from whom He does not expect such a high degree of perfection. From you He expects a surrender of self as proof against all trials and above all, great love.

Your whole heart and soul must be submerged in Him, so that you do nothing except what is His pleasure. Rise above earthly things and your surroundings to lose yourself entirely in His will. You must strive never to lose sight of Him even for a moment. Do not think that for this reason you will be so absorbed as not to be able to attend to your duties. You will experience the very opposite, that the soul most closely united to Jesus will be the one most exact in all her duties, since Jesus, whom she loves, acts for her. He is, so to say, only one with her. Thus you see that she is ably helped and directed in all she has to do.

It is only recollected souls who will have any influence for good around them. Things done differently have no value. The soul that is united to Jesus is the only one that has power over His Heart. She is mistress there and He refuses her nothing. I have many things to tell you on this subject but you would not understand them now. We must wait for the moment willed by God. If you wish it, it will not be long in coming. Jesus has such a great desire to unite Himself entirely to you, more than you can ever understand, and He wishes it more than ever at this moment. Be very attentive in watching over yourself.

It is so delightful to love Jesus, and to be able to pass directly without hindrance from the most intimate earthly union to the far closer union in Heaven. Think well over what I have said to you. One single action of yours, done with purity of intention and offered for my relief, when you are closely united to Jesus, relieves me more than many vocal prayers. The sooner you reach perfection, the quicker will come the day of my deliverance.

It is true that Mother Superior has suffered much these last few days, but one day of great suffering such as she sometimes endures is far more profitable for her soul and for all the community than ten days or more of good health in which she is able to go about and do all the duties of her office.

September 29th. Yes, I did know all the suffering of your Father. That is why, when you asked me if he had gotten over his fatigue, I said, "No," and nothing more. I did not want to worry you. You would have been upset knowing him to be in such sorrow and, as you were thinking of him more than usual before God, evidently by inspiration, I thought it better that he himself should tell you all the heartbreaks he has been enduring. Jesus will remember all of it. The souls he is suffering for are at present in Purgatory but for a short time only. Among them is the priest whom Jesus wants to reward, also those two young men whom He wanted to save, by taking them out of the world where the best can so easily be corrupted. Tell him to be consoled in thinking that Jesus loves him very much and keeps a special place for him in His Sacred Heart, in preference to many others. It is there that he must go in spirit to rest and renew his strength of soul, so as to carry on what he has undertaken to do for His Divine Master.

October 2nd. Say many times a day, "My God, fulfill in me all Thy designs and grant that I may never place any obstacles in the way by any act of mine. My Jesus, I will what Thou willest, because Thou willest it, as Thou willest it, as long as Thou willest it."

Sunday, October 3rd. If only it were given you to understand with what scorn and indifference Jesus is treated on earth, not only by the world in general, but how He is insulted, mocked and held in derision even by those who ought to love Him. Such indifference is found even in religious communities of men and women, His chosen people, where He ought to be treated as a Friend, a Father, a Spouse. Often He does not even receive the consideration shown to a stranger. This indifference is found also among the clergy, at present more than at any other time. He is treated as an equal by those who should tremble at the thought of the awful and august mission with which they have been entrusted. The most sacred reality is often treated with coldness and boredom. How many are there who have the interior spirit? I can assure you that there are but few. Here in Purgatory the priests who are expiating their indifference and their want of love are numerous. Their culpable negligence must be atoned for in the midst of fire and torture of all kinds. You can judge from this that God who is so good and loving to all His creatures finds few who love and console Him.

Alas, there are few. That is the sorrow of the Sacred Heart of Jesus, the ingratitude of His own. Yet His Sacred Heart is full of overflowing love and seeks only to share it. He wants to find some souls bereft of self so as to overpower them with His love, more than He has as yet done for anyone. Oh, how little is Jesus understood on earth, and how little are His mercy and His love understood! People try to seek everything except that which gives real happiness. How pitiable!

You must never be irritated, exteriorly or interiorly. Strive to avoid all annoyances, whether occasioned by the awkwardness or malice of others. Always remain calm. Why get upset because of someone else's fault? It does not improve matters, but rather makes two faults instead of one.

October 14th — During my thanksgiving after Holy Communion. The least infidelity on your part, a slight forgetfulness, the least indifference towards Jesus is very painful to Him and hurts His loving Heart far more than an injury from an enemy. Be very careful in examining yourself, do not omit anything. Let Jesus be able to come with joy to rest in your heart, so that you may be able to console Him for all the griefs with which He is overwhelmed by the world. Act towards Him as to the best of fathers, the most devoted of spouses. Console Him, repair by your love and tenderness the injuries He receives daily. You must take His interests and glory greatly to heart. Forget yourself in His presence and be quite sure that in doing so your interests will become His and He will do far more for you than if you bothered yourself about them.

October 16th. It is useless for you to worry about souls entrusted to you, to reprove them or to try to make them a little more spiritually inclined. You will only succeed in as far as you yourself are spiritual. It is only through the overflow of your own piety that you can put it into their hearts. If you yourself are not what you ought to be, if you are not closely united to Jesus, your words will reach their ears but will not enter into their hearts, and so your efforts will not be fruitful. Do you see how good it is to be united to Jesus? That is the only true happiness on earth.

November 1880. When you have to reprove anyone who has committed a small or even a grave fault, do so with great gentleness. Be firm when the fault demands it, say few words, and never speak when in a passion, for then the reproof will harm the soul of both the one receiving it and the one giving it. Avoid calling attention to former faults, especially when correcting children. This is a common mistake and very displeasing to God, and those who do it are wrong. How do they know that it has not already been pardoned? Then why refer to it again? God has not set us such an example. Our own sins should constantly humble us and we should weep over them in the bitterness of our hearts before the Lord, but we should never refer to the past sins of another.

A Christian soul, and above all a religious soul, to be pleasing in the sight of our Lord, will treat her neighbor as she expects our Lord to treat her. Remember this well and when the opportunity comes, practice it faithfully.

Do not let the duties, cares or worries of life, take so much of your time, so as to prevent you from uniting yourself each moment to Jesus, and from knowing and fulfilling His holy will.

If you have any difficulty, accept it with resignation because it is permitted by Our Lord who, from the evil He permits, knows how to draw the greatest good. Kneel before the Tabernacle and there offer to Jesus the trials of your soul, which at times almost seem unbearable. His Heart will lighten everything. If, on the contrary, you have some joy, especially that happiness which one tastes occasionally in the service of God, accept it in the spirit of humility and gratitude, and remember that the earth is not a place of rest but rather a land of exile, of hard work, and of all kinds of sufferings. Accept all things with a tranquil spirit, letting nothing interfere with your goal. Your only satisfaction, your whole rest must be found in Jesus alone. You must act only for Him, His love must sustain your courage and you can never do enough for so loving a God. The more you detach yourself from earthly things, the more will Jesus shower His choicest graces and Divine caresses upon you. You will often feel quite indifferent to things that formerly attracted you. God in His mercy permits this because He loves you and gradually wants to wean you from material things. That is the way God proceeds with souls that He reserves entirely for Himself. Our Lord permits such souls to become weary of things that are not for His interest, and they experience an aversion for all things that do not serve God's purpose. God permits this to empty their hearts of everything human, so that He may occupy them and fill them with His grace and love.

November. On days when you receive Communion at the first Mass, take only a little breakfast before eight o'clock, say about three minutes. I am telling you this because Our Lord would like you to prolong your thanksgiving. This would give you an extra quarter of an hour, besides your usual quarter, and you would then have more time to converse with Jesus since you have so many things to tell Him. And so the second quarter would be spent for Him alone. Continue in like manner during the Little Hours and during the greater part of the Mass. Ask Mother Superior›s permission to do this. How many more graces you would receive! By a special favor the Sacred Species remain with you after Communion for a long time. Spend these happy moments in heartfelt gratitude with Him whom Heaven itself cannot contain. Thus you can obtain all that your heart desires. What love God thus shows to His poor creature, to lower Himself so as to be able to commune with her as friend to friend. During these moments, adore, thank and beg Him for help, above all make reparation for the injuries that Jesus receives from this ungrateful world of ours. He is so offended. Do love Him well. You know that He loves you. There is sufficient proof for it.

While you are still on earth, it is impossible to understand what God demands of a soul expiating its sins in Purgatory. You are under the impression that many prayers, well said, will place a soul almost at once in possession of eternal happiness. It is nothing of the kind. Who can fathom the judgments of God? Who can understand how pure a soul must be before He admits it to share His eternal happiness? Alas, if people only knew, if they would only consider it while still on earth, what different lives they would lead!

Seriously reflect how many venial sins one who is careless about her eternal salvation commits in one day.

How many minutes does she offer up to God? Does she think of Him seriously at all? Well, there are 365 days in one year, and if there are many such years, that person dies charged with a multitude of venial sins which have not been blotted out because she has not even thought of them.

When such a soul appears before God to be judged there is scarcely a spark of love left in that soul when she comes to render an account of her life to Him who demands it back from her. Such all but sterile lives have to be begun all over again, when they reach this place of expiation. Lives lived without love for God will have to be atoned for here in Purgatory with intense sufferings. Whilst on earth, they did not profit by the mercy of God, but lived merely for the sake of the body. Now to regain their first splendor, they have to make satisfaction to the last farthing. That is what happens to indifferent souls. For souls of greater guilt, it is far worse.

Try to love God now so much that you will not have to come here in order to learn how to love Him through sufferings which are without merit. The sufferings and trials on earth are meritorious, therefore, do not lose one of them — but above all, love. Love wipes out many faults and makes one avoid them so as not to give pain to the One we love. That is why a soul that really loves Jesus is constantly on its guard to avoid everything that would grieve His Divine Heart. There are many souls in Purgatory depending on you to deliver them from this place of suffering. Pray with all your heart for them.

1881. To be a friend of Jesus on earth entails suffering of body and soul. The more He loves a soul, the more He shares with it the sorrow He endured for us. Happy is the soul thus privileged. What an opportunity for merit! That is the short cut to Heaven. So do not shun suffering, rather welcome it, since it unites you more intimately with Him, whom you truly love. Have I not told you before that love makes everything sweet? Sorrows appear bitter because you do not love enough. The infallible means of arriving quickly at close union with Jesus is love, but love united to suffering. You have had up to this time many crosses and yet you do not love them as Jesus wants you to.

If only you were aware how beneficial sufferings are for the soul! They are the most tender caresses which the Divine Spouse can give to her whom He wishes to unite more closely to Himself. He sends to that favored soul cross upon cross, suffering upon suffering, in order to detach it from this world. Then He can speak to her heart. What passes during these celestial communications! You would know if you only desired it. Jesus is holding back all the graces which He will pour upon you, until He sees you prepared and fit to receive them. Our Lord wishes you to act for Him alone and to direct all your actions to His greatest glory, to make Him the confidant of all your joys and sorrows. Do not do the least thing without asking for His advice and guidance, and wish for no other recompense in all you do than just His love alone. You attempted to do this several years ago! You then said to Him, "My Jesus, may I never meet with any gratitude on earth for the little good I may do. You alone are enough for me." How does this request appear to you now? Has it been fulfilled? Jesus never allows Himself to be outdone in generosity. You will experience that. You may know also that it is not so much your prayers that will obtain eternal joy for me, as will your actions done perfectly and in close union with Jesus. Be assured that He had great designs for your soul when He sent me to you in this way. If I could only tell you all that I know regarding this matter. How great is the love of Jesus for you! What kindness, what consideration He has shown you, and He is not discouraged by your indifference. How cold and forgetful you are sometimes towards so good a God!

Ask His pardon for all these shortcomings and respect Him as the most loving Father. Do not fear to importune Him. I like to see more confidence in your soul. Always try to please Him, from the time you awake in the morning until night, without ever listening to your own nature.

April 1881. If you are not advancing more quickly in perfection, it is because your will is not united closely enough with that of God.

Jesus submits patiently to all these delays, but who is the loser? You are. If you only knew what graces Jesus is storing up for you, how He longs to be united to you, you would give up your rebellious will which submits to Him today but does not do so again on the morrow. He who is so good and so loving is asking this of you.

Jesus will not let you rest until you arrive at that perfection He has destined for you. You may do as you
like, but until your will is united with that of Jesus and
your actions are performed under His direction and
for His pleasure, you will have neither peace, nor rest,
nor happiness of soul.

September 1882. Jesus has done very much for you and
He will do still more for you in the future, but you
must correspond with His graces in a generous spirit.
The souls that arrive at the height of perfection that
He demands of them are mistresses of His Heart. He
refuses them nothing. When you will have arrived at
that stage, Jesus and yourself will be but one. Your
sentiments, your thoughts and your desires will be the
same. Be good, therefore, make haste to become a saint
to procure great glory for your one Friend who waits
for that moment to inundate your soul with His grace.
You do not yet make sufficient effort in watching
over your interior and in keeping before your mind
the Divine Presence of Jesus. Try to take trouble and
you will be powerfully helped. Jesus is only waiting
for a little good will on your part and He will do the
rest. Say to yourself every day, "Since Jesus began to
give me so many special graces, what have I become?
What ought I to be? What would I be if I had always
corresponded well?" These thoughts meditated on for
a few minutes will do much good to your soul. Only
reflect seriously on them, for it is the will of God that I
have told you. He also desires that you work seriously
at your perfection because upon it depends that of
many others. Jesus has such an intense love for you that

He desires to pour upon you His choice graces which He shares only with His intimate friends. Hasten by your prayers and sacrifices the happy moment which will witness the Divine union that Jesus wishes to form with your soul.

Acknowledge before this Divine Friend your own poverty and the abyss of your miseries and then let Him act as He wills. This is the way of His love, to enrich the most miserable. His goodness is then shown forth to advantage. Try to love Jesus very much! Cling to Him more firmly than to anything else, join yourself to Him with the strength of your heart so that you may live only for His love.

For the love of Jesus love all those who live with you and those with whom you have any dealings. Do not be afraid to make an effort to be amiable towards them, to pray for them and to deny yourself out of regard for them. The more a soul loves Jesus the more she loves her neighbor.

October 30th. You are always complaining because you say you would rather be like everyone else, but you have not done with me yet. You will have to listen to me as long as God wills it. You may try as hard as you can to get rid of me but I have still many things to say to you. Perhaps some day you will understand all this better.

December 25th. Do not be unhappy because I am not yet in Heaven. It is true that I said, "I shall only enter Heaven when you have arrived at the perfection God demands of you." However, the high degree of perfection to which Jesus is calling you is not attained in such a short time. There are different degrees of perfection and it is not the lowest one that is demanded of you. You know that Jesus loves you in spite of the fact that you are very far from that state to which He has called you. This beloved Friend knows that it would require a miracle to arrive (immediately) at the state of perfection to which He calls some souls and He will not perform that miracle.

The soul must advance on the narrow path, often so difficult to human nature. To attain the goal which Jesus has planned for you, you must become entirely dead to self and have no longer any will of your own nor love of self. As yet, you are not there. Thus if someone accuses you wrongly and attributes to you motives you never had (you know of what I am speaking) you should not let it vex you. It is God who permits this to give you the opportunity to renounce yourself and cling only to Him. He wishes you to arrive at that state where nothing whatsoever can disturb the peace of your soul. Sorrows, joys, disappointments, all should pass by unheeded. Listen well, God wishes to fulfill all your desires, to satiate your heart and be your all in all and, believe me, this is not the work of a day.

No, you are not too indulgent. In some cases it is far better to yield than to keep the upper hand. Here is a point in question that Jesus wants you to follow. Before giving advice or a well merited reproof to a pupil or anyone else, recollect yourself for a moment, then put yourself in the other person's place and act toward her as you would want her to act toward you in a similar situation. Then Jesus will be pleased.

1883. Again, another year has passed into eternity! In like manner others will pass by, days follow each other until the one that puts an end to the short days of life on earth, and then begins the long life of eternity. Use every minute well, as each one of them is an opportunity to merit Heaven and escape Purgatory. Every action performed in the presence of Jesus merits an extra degree of glory in Heaven and a greater love for Him. Your actions thus performed forge a chain of love that unites the soul closer and closer to its Beloved. When the last link has been completed, Jesus breaks the feeble bonds that keep the soul, now full of merit, in the body, and it becomes united with Him for all eternity. Thus you understand how a life spent in the gradual absorption of the soul with Christ can really be a happy one. If in a few minutes, the soul can be elevated in ecstatic union with Jesus and forget all its past sufferings, what must a union of eternity be like? Oh, if you could only know! If you could understand it! You, to whom Jesus has given every possible means of attaining it, would work at your perfection without ceasing. Oh, if we here had only five minutes of the time that you waste thinking about yourself and wondering if what I say to you is true or false, what we, in turn, would do for Him for whom we yearn so ardently! It is the devil who blinds you sometimes and makes you disregard what I say. He knows well what the result would be. Avoid his tricks, throw yourself wholeheartedly into the work of your sanctification and let this year be the beginning of that perfect life that Jesus has been expecting from you all this while. Right at the beginning of this year, take as your practice not to say one useless word, do not express your opinion unless obliged to do so, speak little and do not raise your eyes out of curiosity. Your first look in the morning should be directed toward Jesus, your first thought for Him, and your first word, one of thanksgiving and love. Then at the foot of the altar, place your heart in that of Jesus for the whole day, and in spirit, speak with Him there until evening. Again in the evening, place yourself at the feet of Jesus with true sorrow for your faults and genuine thanksgiving for His graces. You remember what I have said to you on this subject. Be very faithful in these practices. Jesus wants from you an unlimited purity of intention. Do not spare yourself anything, the more a soul sacrifices herself the happier she is. It is a known fact that love is repaid by love, but love is also repaid by gratitude, the denial of self and the gift of oneself. Therefore, you must sacrifice yourself and offer yourself without reserve. Suffering always prepares the way for love. There is a degree of love which only those attain who have suffered much and suffered well, and in this, I mean mainly the sufferings of the soul. The greatest suffering that a soul really loving Jesus can endure is that of not being able to love Him as much as she desires.

Oh, how much Jesus loves you in spite of your coldness and misery. Recall all the graces He bestowed upon you, how He drew you to Himself by kindness, suffering and trials. He detaches you from yourself and by love He desires to unite you so closely to Himself that you might become as it were *"Another Jesus"*.

Mother — is in the lowest Purgatory. Souls of religious, priests and those on whom graces have been showered have a terrible Purgatory if they abuse the means which God has placed at their disposal.

May 1883 — Retreat. When God desires something special from a soul He has many ways of achieving it. His plans are well laid out and kept. He makes Himself known on the great day when it pleases Him. It is for you especially that Jesus has from all eternity decreed to prepare and sanctify the person of whom I spoke to you. You will sanctify each other. God loves you and you love Him.

During this retreat your union must be still closer. Your love must increase, your will must be one with that of Jesus and His interests must be yours. Why do you worry yourself about your Father? All that God does is well done. Is it not He who has prepared and given him to you? Why should He take him away? The ways of God are impenetrable. What will He not do to unite Himself to a soul that He wishes to be His alone? What unknown ways He has in His power! So be very trustful of your Jesus; do not doubt His goodness. The better you are the more you will try to please Him in every way and the more generous He will be to you.

This retreat must be the beginning of that high stage of perfection to which Jesus has been calling you for so long. Jesus expects much from this retreat. He has given you a new special grace. What more do you want? In return give yourself without reserve. Let Him be the Master of your heart. Watch very carefully over your soul. Let your communication with Jesus always be heart to heart.

Let no word, no thought, not even a desire come from you that is not according to His adorable Will. If you only knew what that union is that Jesus wishes to contract with your soul, you would never put any hindrance in the way. Neither would you kick against the goad as you do. At last do you understand? This height of perfection is scaring you, as you think you are being deceived. But with Jesus, why should you fear? He is your Father, your Friend, your Spouse, your All. Has He not the right to demand what He wills from a soul without telling it why? He is the great Master, the Lord of all. Why do you try with your limited vision to examine His conduct? Adore His designs and obey blindly. This is what He demands of you, therefore, with all your heart, work seriously at your sanctification. Renew your love and tenderness for Jesus. Console Him, try to make up to Him for all the affronts He receives in the world. Love Him for all those who do not think of doing so. Jesus expects this of you; will you refuse Him?

May 20th. Jesus gives proof of His love for you, but in return He demands proof of your love for Him. You are aware of all He is asking from you; you must no longer hesitate. Give yourself entirely to Him. Bury yourself in Him and never recall the gift. On earth we manage our own affairs, but in the next world, God arranges for us as He thinks fit. There are but few real friendships on earth. Often people love each other from caprice or self-interest. Then a little coldness, a word, a want of attention separates friends who seemed inseparable. That is because God is not in possession of their souls; only hearts that are overflowing with the love of Jesus can give of their superabundance to their friends. All friendship that is not rooted in God is false and is not lasting. But when Jesus takes possession of a heart, it can love and do good to its friends, because it has in it the source of pure and unalloyed friendship. All the rest is human and nothing else. Always have a higher aim than those of the earth, which is worldliness.

Never seek the esteem or the friendship of anyone. Jesus alone is yours and He wishes you to be His forever. Your heart is not too large for Him. Love Him alone.

June 1883. Well, are you satisfied? Will you now believe me? I forgive you all that you have been thinking about me these last days. Under the circumstances, it could not be otherwise. You have committed no sin. Look at the kindness of Jesus; after having allowed the devil to make you suffer so much, He finally vanquished him and His Holy Will was accomplished. That is what He is waiting for. When God has special designs on a soul, they are not fulfilled without much suffering. You have proven this once more, have you not? But you were not alone.

M. L. must never permit himself to be discouraged. There may come moments of worry and fatigue, but he has the Tabernacle, let him there open his heart to

Jesus and ask with great confidence for light so that he may be a light to the souls confided to his care. Jesus loves him and will prove it to him. In return, he can never do enough for so good a God.

June 1883. Are you not happy in finally having found a spiritual Father? Pay great attention to all he says to you and you will greatly please God. This is another grace, so profit well by it. It is a great fortune for a soul to meet a director that understands her. That is indeed rare on earth. Jesus meets with such few generous souls on earth; there are so few who love Him, even among His priests. The good Master hopes for much from your Father. Oh, how great a priest is! What a sublime mission is his but, alas, in these days there are few who understand this.

August 28, 1883 — Feast of St. Augustine. So far, you have never prayed as Jesus wants you to pray. You do not pay enough attention to His inspirations, and you often lose sight of His presence which is the cause of your not advancing in perfection as He has planned for you. Watch carefully, therefore, over your interior. I have been asking this of you in His Name for such a long time.

August 29th — Retreat. For many years God has been pursuing you, but on one pretext or another you have always turned a deaf ear. It is high time that you should begin to pay attention to all that I have told you. Profit by these holy days of the retreat and put into practice all you have written down. See how you stand with Jesus who is so good and so patient with you.

Remember, He might grow weary of you in the end, seeing that you make so little account of the graces He has already given you and those He has still in store for you in the future. Once and for all, show Jesus that you do really love Him and give up your will to Him. There have been enough hesitations. Tell Him that He may do what He wills with you, but this must come from the bottom of your heart. To arrive at sanctity is not so difficult as you imagine. You suffer more in resisting and struggling every day against God, who is drawing you to Himself, than you would if you definitely gave yourself to Him without reserve.

7:00 o'clock. Accustom yourself to speak to our Lord as to your most sincere and devoted friend. Neither do or say anything without consulting Him. You have been told this repeatedly during many years past and I have also told it to you. Today, I repeat it once more. God wants you to pay attention to it and above all to put it into practice. This glance of your soul towards Jesus, so as to catch each slightest wish, together with the colloquies He wishes to have with you, will not disturb you and will never prevent you from discharging your exterior occupations well. On the contrary, it is impossible to be calm and recollected if the interior is not so. This is what Jesus asks of you, a life of faith and perpetual union with Him, a humble, hidden life known to Him alone. Let Jesus be everything to you. Regard everything as a means which He makes use of so as to unite Himself ever more closely to you, and thus to accomplish His designs on you. Do not put any obstacles in the way; be generous, sparing neither energy nor good will. So start this life of self-denial, of sacrifice and above all of love, which Jesus is determined to obtain from you. Thus only will you find the peace and calm which He has been offering to you for so many years.

Let the Holy Will of God be the foundation of all that you may have to do or suffer. Jesus expects much from you, much suffering of soul and body, and especially your love. It is impossible to love without suffering. This you know well and you have had abundant proof of it in the past. Prepare yourself for what is to come in the future. God has endowed you with the ability to suffer more than anyone else. This is a grace and an act of mercy to you. When there are great sacrifices to be made there is more merit. I plead with you not to resist any longer the designs which God has in regard to you. Do not ask for any further proofs — you have experienced enough. You know well that Jesus wants you to be entirely His. Weigh all these things at the foot of the Tabernacle, ask Him for His guidance and do not delay any longer to carry out His plans. Ask Him for His help, first of all for yourself, and then for other souls.

Some day you will have to answer for all these privileges. All for Jesus! Pay no attention to what others may think of you. The devil is stirring this up to stop your spiritual progress and Jesus allows it to detach you from all that surrounds you. Let your one object always be to carry out all your duties and perform all your actions for love of Jesus. This is all that matters, the rest is secondary. Be very generous, put your *Ego* behind you and put Jesus in front of you. Think often of this if you want your actions to be pleasing to Jesus. There must be a little sacrifice in each one of them, something that costs you an effort. Without that there is no merit. Surely it is not difficult for you above all people to please Jesus. No longer think that when anything costs you a great deal of effort that there is no merit in it. The very opposite is the truth. Let only Jesus and yourself know about it. Ask me every evening if God is pleased with you and I will tell you how you stand. You have suffered much and you will suffer still more but in exchange Jesus has been good to you and He has a lot more in store for you in the future.

May 1886. It is true that no one merits graces from God. They are His gifts, and when He bestows them we are to receive them with gratitude and profit by them. For the soul of a religious, the interior spirit of recollection is essential, also a life of sacrifice and purity of intention. This is the sum total of religious life. Learn to respect the Rule and Priests. Those who attack the ministers of Jesus Christ wound Him seriously, as they are the apple of His eye. Woe, three times woe, to any man or woman who acts in this manner.

It is more pleasing to God for a religious to perform all her actions in conscious union with Him and with a pure intention in behalf of her deceased relatives rather than to say many prayers for them.

It is the soul that God loves most that He crucifies on earth, but this cross sent by God has always a certain sweetness mingled with its bitterness. It is not so with the crosses that come to us through our own fault; in them we find unmixed bitterness.

November 1886. You talk about these trials! Well, God has permitted them as a trial and thus He has given you strength of soul to make His glory, justice and love triumph. He desires a life of union with Him, a life of reparation and prayer. If you will take these interests of Jesus to heart He will also share in yours.

Christmas 1886. If you just wanted to you could soon be rid of me and I would be delivered from Purgatory.

February 1887. When God has any particular designs on a person, when He wishes her to be out of the ordinary, He gives her a magnanimous soul, a generous heart, a sound judgment and a level head. When you do not meet with these qualities or characteristics in anyone, it means that God does not expect anything out of the ordinary from him.

Jesus does not make known to a soul at once what He requires of her. She would be terrified. Little by little as His grace makes her stronger, He reveals His secrets to her and He makes her a partner in His crucifixion. God loves you in a special manner. You are His daughter of predilection. All that has happened to you was for your greater good. Everyone must love God intensely but for you it is a special obligation. You must reciprocate.

June 24th. Remain closely united to Jesus. Before every action, however trivial, or whatever you may have to do or say, ask His advice. Speak to Him heart to heart as to a friend whom one has always close at hand. Jesus wants your whole soul with all its faculties and powers, your heart with all its affections, all its love. The good Jesus wants to be one with you and all the graces and devotedness you require for others, you should draw from His Sacred Heart, that Divine Source which can never be exhausted. This is how spouses who love each other should act, and you especially whom He loves above all. Jesus desires that you render Him an equal love. Oh, if I could only tell you all the graces God has in store for you if you do not put any obstacles in the way of His actions; compelling graces which would bind you irrevocably to Him, choice, rare and deep graces and trusts. He has many things to confide to you for yourself alone, as well as for the common good.

Whenever you can pass by the church, make a little visit to Jesus and pour out the love of your heart to Him. Tell Him all your sorrows, your joys, your sufferings, in one word, everything. Speak to Him as to a loving Friend, a Father, a Spouse. Tell Him of all your tender love for Him, and when you cannot go to church, speak to Him in your heart. From time to time, during the day, fill your mind for a few minutes with the Divine Presence, recollect yourself before His Majesty, acknowledging your own misery but also His goodness and thank Him affectionately. All the day long you can speak to Jesus heart to heart. That is what He expects from you and what He has been waiting for so long.

If you are faithful to all I tell you, if you take the trouble to try to please your Jesus in everything, if you give to Him all the little loving attentions of a devoted heart, always on the lookout to please her spouse, Jesus on His part will keep for you His most secret communications, His Divine caresses, His most tender love as a Father and Spouse and He will refuse you nothing. If you give yourself entirely to Him, He will give Himself entirely to you. God wishes that this retreat should establish in you a state in which He has desired to see you for ever so long a time.

God attains His ends by ways often unknown to us. Set yourself to work well, seriously and courageously. On His side Jesus is about to give you new graces. Respond to them generously for your own sake and for the good of the community.

Permit Jesus to bend and mold you as He pleases. Listen attentively to His voice in the depth of your soul and do not lose one of His graces. Let your will be one with His adorable will and let your heart be lost in His. He will soon accomplish His designs in you if you do not place any obstacles in His way. Do not lose sight of His Divine Presence. God wishes you to be extraordinarily holy and to belong to Him alone. If only you would take the trouble to do this. Above all things, Jesus desires to find in your heart love that is pure, disinterested, generous; love that does not fear suffering nor seek its own ease. All this is to be done with the sole object of pleasing Jesus alone.

God does not forbid us to take care of our bodies, but there are some people whom He Himself wishes to nurse and cure whenever He thinks it proper to do so. For such, remedies do not help. A little mortification is better for them than anything else. Believe what I say to you — you will see that it is true.

A common life, that is what Jesus wants of you whom He cherishes so intimately. Let practical faith animate all your actions and let your trust in Jesus and His love make you undertake generously all that He requires of you. Every morning on awakening say to your Beloved: "My Jesus, I am ready to accomplish Your Will — what do You want me to do to please You today?" Perform all your exercises of piety with great love in the presence of Jesus. You can do good for souls only in proportion as you are united to God. God is seeking for souls to repair the outrages which He receives; souls that love Him and make Him loved by others. He wants you to be of this number.

At a given moment, God unmasks the plots and defeats the plans of those who do not act solely for His glory.

Before allowing a soul such intimate union with Himself, Jesus purifies it by trials, and the greater his designs on a soul, all the greater are the trials. The devil sees very well that God has special designs on you, that is why he harasses you so much and causes you to be worried by his agents. Do not be discouraged. God is helping you and will help you. Fight with great courage — in spite of the efforts of Hell, God will achieve His goal. God makes use of me to encourage you because you have no one else. Remember that and see how human nature has need of these little encouragements. Think of this when the occasion arrives, since you have, and will continue to have, charge of souls.

God gives you an example of this in the Agony in the Garden. Have entire confidence in Jesus, He will never fail you. Fix your habitual dwelling place in the Heart of Jesus. Let love be the chain which unites your heart to His adorable Heart.

Your heart which is so miserable will be purified and become detached by contact with His pure Heart. Draw also from the Divine Heart of Jesus all the graces you need for others and for your charges. He will refuse you nothing that you ask of Him with confidence and love. The trials and sufferings of the soul are more acute than those of the body. But for souls that love Jesus, the greatest sorrow is to know that they cause Him pain daily by their sins and ingratitude. Ask from the Heart of Jesus for that strength that is necessary for you that He may be able to work out His designs in you.

If God requires such great purity in a soul that He admits into Heaven, it is because He is the Eternal Purity, Beauty and Justice, the Eternal Goodness and Perfection.

God permits that you should thus suffer in body and soul that He may be able to fulfill in you all His great designs, in order that you may know the art of perfecting others by your own experience.

In order to fix your mind firmly on the presence of God, take each day one of the fourteen Stations of Our Lord in His Passion and dwell on it more particularly. Jesus wishes that we recall all the sufferings He has endured for us. On feast days, meditate in like manner on one of the glorious mysteries, e.g., the Resurrection, the Ascension, etc. Think often on the Holy Eucharist, on the hidden life of Jesus in the Tabernacle. There, above all, you will see His love concealed, alone and waiting in vain for someone to come and say to Him, "Jesus, I love You." Every Sunday make your little plan for the week ahead, in one word, seek to please Jesus and He will repay you in the same measure. By Holy Communion, Jesus will unite you to Himself most intimately — more so than He has ever done to anyone before. You will find in this Divine Food an extraordinary strength to raise you up to the height of perfection that Jesus requires of you.

All things pass and pass quickly. Do not fret so much about things that will end one day. Aim at what will never end. By our holy actions united to Jesus, let us embellish our heavenly throne. Let us raise it up a few steps nearer to Him whom we shall contemplate and love throughout eternity.

This is what should be our sole concern on earth. For a soul that He loves, Jesus does things that at first seem impossible. That is how He will act toward you. It is Jesus who is drawing you to Himself sweetly and gently but at the same time strongly and perseveringly. Do not refuse His Divine attraction.

In a short time Jesus will tell you what He requires of you. In the meantime, it is I whom He charges to make known to you His Divine Will. Listen well to His voice which is speaking to you in the secret depths of your heart. Refuse Him nothing and you will gain everything, because if you are generous He will be much more so. You already have had proof of this many times.

God wants in His service generous souls who have no thought of themselves, but who direct all their attention and good will to making Him loved and who serve Him at the expense of their own interests. God's graces are pure gifts which He does not owe us. He gives them to whomsoever He pleases without anyone having the right to question Him about it. Who has the right to lay down the law to the Divine Master? Therefore, receive in all humility and gratitude the special graces with which Jesus favors you, without trying to understand the why and the wherefore. Jesus wishes you to soar above all that is created so that not one bond or thread binds you to earth. You must live the life of the elect, whose only occupation is to enjoy, love and lose themselves entirely in God Himself.

November 2, 1890 — A Remembrance. This is the last Benediction of the month of the Rosary.

I am going to try to make you understand, as far as you can upon earth, what Heaven is like. There are ever new feasts which succeed each other without interruption. There is happiness, always new and such, it would seem, as has never been enjoyed. It is a torrent of joy which flows unceasingly over the elect. Heaven is above all and beyond all — GOD: God loved, God relished, God delighted in; in one word, it is to be satisfied with God without ever being satisfied!

The more a soul loves God on earth, the higher she advances in perfection, the more she will love and understand God in Heaven.

Jesus is the true joy upon earth and the eternal felicity of Heaven.

END

Treatise on Purgatory

St. Catherine of Genoa

Contents

CHAPTER XVI

This Soul shews again how the sufferings of the souls in Purgatory are no hindrance at all to their peace and their joy.

CHAPTER XVII

She concludes by applying all she has said of the souls in Purgatory to what she feels, and has proved in her own soul.

Nihil Obstat: Ernestus C. Messenger, Ph.D

Censor Deputatus Imprimatur: E. Morrogh Bernard
Vic. Gen.Westmonasterii, die 18 Decembris 1945

Treatise on Purgatory[*]

CHAPTER I

The state of the souls who are in Purgatory, how they are exempt from all self-love.

This holy Soul found herself, while still in the flesh, placed by the fiery love of God in Purgatory, which burnt her, cleansing whatever in her needed cleansing, to the end that when she passed from this life she might be presented to the sight of God, her dear Love. By means of this loving fire, she understood in her soul the state of the souls of the faithful who are placed in Purgatory to purge them of all the rust and stains of sin of which they have not rid themselves in this life. And since this Soul, placed by the divine fire in this loving Purgatory, was united to that divine love and content with all that was wrought in her, she understood the state of the souls who are in Purgatory. And she said:

The souls who are in Purgatory cannot, as I understand, choose but be there, and this is by God's ordinance who therein has done justly. They cannot turn their thoughts back to themselves, nor can they say, "Such sins I have committed for which I deserve to be

* The chapter headings and all references to Catherine as "holy" were undoubtedly added by an editor.

here", nor, "I would that I had not committed them for then I would go now to Paradise", nor, "That one will leave sooner than I", nor, "I will leave sooner than he". They can have neither of themselves nor of others any memory, whether of good or evil, whence they would have greater pain than they suffer ordinarily. So happy are they to be within God's ordinance, and that He should do all which pleases Him, as it pleases Him that in their greatest pain they cannot think of themselves. They see only the working of the divine goodness, which leads man to itself mercifully, so that he no longer sees aught of the pain or good which may befall him. Nor would these souls be in pure charity if they could see that pain or good. They cannot see that they are in pain because of their sins; that sight they cannot hold in their minds because in it there would be an active imperfection, which cannot be where no actual sin can be.

Only once, as they pass from this life, do they see the cause of the Purgatory they endure; never again do they see it for in another sight of it there would be self. Being then in charity from which they cannot now depart by any actual fault, they can no longer will nor desire save with the pure will of pure charity. Being in that fire of Purgatory, they are within the divine ordinance, which is pure charity, and in nothing can they depart thence for they are deprived of the power to sin as of the power to merit.

CHAPTER II

What is the joy of the souls in Purgatory. A comparison to shew how they see God ever more and more. The difficulty of speaking of this state.

I believe no happiness can be found worthy to be compared with that of a soul in Purgatory except that of the saints in Paradise; and day by day this happiness grows as God flows into these souls, more and more as the hindrance to His entrance is consumed. Sin's rust is the hindrance, and the fire burns the rust away so that more and more the soul opens itself up to the divine inflowing. A thing which is covered cannot respond to the sun's rays, not because of any defect in the sun, which is shining all the time, but because the cover is an obstacle; if the cover be burnt away, this thing is open to the sun; more and more as the cover is consumed does it respond to the rays of the sun.

It is in this way that rust, which is sin, covers souls, and in Purgatory is burnt away by fire; the more it is consumed, the more do the souls respond to God, the true sun. As the rust lessens and the soul is opened up to the divine ray, happiness grows; until the time be accomplished the one wanes and the other waxes. Pain however does not lessen but only the time for which pain is endured. As for will: never can the souls say these pains are pains, so contented are they with God's ordaining with which, in pure charity, their will is united.

But, on the other hand, they endure a pain so extreme that no tongue can be found to tell it, nor could the mind understand its least pang if God by special grace did not shew so much. Which least pang God of His grace shewed to this Soul, but with her tongue she cannot say what it is. This sight which the Lord revealed to me has never since left my mind and I will tell what I can of it. They will understand whose mind God deigns to open.

CHAPTER III

Separation from God is the chief punishment of Purgatory. Wherein Purgatory differs from Hell.

All the pains of Purgatory arise from original or actual sin. God created the soul pure, simple and clean of all stain of sin, with a certain beatific instinct towards Himself whence original sin, which the soul finds in itself, draws it away, and when actual is added to original sin the soul is drawn yet further away. The further it departs from its beatific instinct, the more malignant it becomes because it corresponds less to God.

There can be no good save by participation in God, who meets the needs of irrational creatures as He wills and has ordained, never failing them, and answers to a rational soul in the measure in which He finds it cleansed of sin's hindrance. When therefore a soul has come near to the pure and clear state in which it was created, its beatific instinct discovers itself and grows unceasingly, so impetuously and with such fierce charity (drawing it to its last end) that any hindrance seems to this soul a thing past bearing. The more it sees, the more extreme is its pain.

Because the souls in Purgatory are without the guilt of sin, there is no hindrance between them and God except their pain, which holds them back so that they cannot reach perfection. Clearly they see the grievousness of every least hindrance in their way, and see too that their instinct is hindered by a necessity of justice: thence is born a raging fire, like that of Hell save that guilt is lacking to it. Guilt it is which makes the will of the damned in Hell malignant, on whom God does not bestow His goodness and who remain therefore in desperate ill will, opposed to the will of God.

CHAPTER IV

Of the state of the souls in Hell and of the difference between them and those in Purgatory. Reflections of this saint on those who are careless of their salvation.

Hence it is manifest that there is perversity of will, contrary to the will of God, where the guilt is known and ill will persists, and that the guilt of those who have passed with ill will from this life to Hell is not remitted, nor can be since they may no longer change the will with which they have passed out of this life, in which passage the soul is made stable in good or evil in accordance with its deliberate will. As it is written, "*Ubi te invenero*", that is in the hour of death, with the will to sin or dissatisfaction with sin or repentance for sin, "*Ibi te judicabo*." Of which judgment there is afterwards no remission, as I will shew:

After death free will can never return, for the will is fixed as it was at the moment of death. Because the souls in Hell were found at the moment of death to have in them the will to sin, they bear the guilt throughout eternity, suffering not indeed the pains they merit but such pains as they endure, and these without end. But the souls in Purgatory bear only pain, for their guilt was wiped away at the moment of their death when they were found to be ill content with their sins and repentant for their offences against divine goodness. Therefore their pain is finite and its time ever lessening, as has been said.

O misery beyond all other misery, the greater that human blindness takes it not into account!

The pain of the damned is not infinite in quantity because the dear goodness of God sheds the ray of His mercy even in Hell. For man dead in sin merits infinite pain for an infinite time, but God's mercy has allotted infinity to him only in time and has determined the quantity of his pain; in justice God could have given him more pain.

O how dangerous is sin committed in malice! Hardly does a man repent him thereof, and without repentance he will bear its guilt for as long as he perseveres, that is for as long as he wills a sin committed or wills to sin again.

CHAPTER V

Of the peace and the joy there are in Purgatory.

The souls in Purgatory have wills accordant in all things with the will of God, who therefore sheds on them His goodness, and they, as far as their will goes, are happy and cleansed of all their sin. As for guilt, these cleansed souls are as they were when God created them, for God forgives their guilt immediately who have passed from this life ill content with their sins, having confessed all they have committed and having the will to commit no more. Only the rust of sin is left them and from this they cleanse themselves by pain in the fire. Thus cleansed of all guilt and united in will to God, they see Him clearly in the degree in which He makes Himself known to them, and see too how much it imports to enjoy Him and that souls have been created for this end. Moreover, they are brought to so uniting a conformity with God, and are drawn to Him in such wise, His natural instinct towards souls working in them, that neither arguments nor figures nor examples can make the thing clear as the mind knows it to be in effect and as by inner feeling it is understood to be. I will, however, make one comparison which comes to my mind.

CHAPTER VI

A comparison to shew with what violence and what love the souls in Purgatory desire to enjoy God.

If in all the world there were but one loaf of bread to feed the hunger of all creatures, and if they were satisfied by the sight of it alone, then since man, if he be healthy, has an instinct to eat, his hunger, if he neither ate nor sickened nor died, would grow unceasingly for his instinct to eat would not lessen. Knowing that there was only that loaf to satisfy him and that without it he must still be hungry, he would be in unbearable pain.

All the more if he went near that loaf and could not see it, would his natural craving for it be strengthened; his instinct would fix his desire wholly on that loaf which held all that could content him; at this point, if he were sure he would never see the loaf again, he would be in Hell. Thus are the souls of the damned from whom any hope of ever seeing their bread, which is God, the true Savior, has been taken away. But the souls in Purgatory have the hope of seeing their bread and wholly satisfying themselves therewith. Therefore they suffer hunger and endure pain in that measure in which they will be able to satisfy themselves with the bread which is Jesus Christ, true God and Savior and our Love.

CHAPTER VII

Of God's admirable wisdom in making Purgatory and Hell.

As the clean and purified spirit can find rest only in God, having been created for this end, so there is no place save Hell for the soul in sin, for whose end Hell was ordained by God. When the soul as it leaves the body is in mortal sin, then, in the instant in which spirit and body are separated, the soul goes to the place ordained for it, unguided save by the nature of its sin. And if at that moment the soul were bound by no ordinance proceeding from God's justice, it would go to a yet greater hell than that in which it abides, for it would be outside His ordinance, in which divine mercy has part so that God gives the soul less pain than it deserves. The soul, finding no other place to hand nor any holding less evil for it, casts itself by God's ordinance into Hell as into its proper place.

To return to our matter which is the Purgatory of the soul separated from the body when it is no longer clean as it was created. Seeing in itself the impediment which can be taken away only by means of Purgatory, it casts itself therein swiftly and willingly. Were there not the ordinance it thus obeys, one fit to rid it of its encumbrance, it would in that instant beget within itself a hell worse than Purgatory, for it would see that because of that impediment it could not draw near to God, its end. So much does God import that Purgatory in comparison counts not at all. Even for all that it is, as has been said, like Hell, because compared to God, it appears almost nothing.

CHAPTER VIII

Of the necessity of Purgatory. How terrible it is.

When I look at God, I see no gate to Paradise, and yet because God is all mercy he who wills enters there. God stands before us with open arms to receive us into His glory. But well I see the divine essence to be of such purity, greater far than can be imagined, that the soul in which there is even the least note of imperfection would rather cast itself into a thousand Hells than find itself thus stained in the presence of the Divine Majesty. Therefore the soul, understanding that Purgatory has been ordained to take away those stains, casts itself therein, and seems to itself to have found great mercy in that it can rid itself there of the impediment which is the stain of sin.

No tongue can tell nor explain, no mind understand, the grievousness of Purgatory. But I, though I see that there is in Purgatory as much pain as in Hell, yet see the soul which has the least stain of imperfection accepting Purgatory, as I have said, as though it were a mercy, and holding its pains of no account as compared with the least stain which hinders a soul in its love. I seem to see that the pain which souls in Purgatory endure because of whatever in them displeases God, that is what they have willfully done against His so great goodness, is greater than any other pain they feel in Purgatory. And this is because, being in grace, they see the truth and the grievousness of the hindrance which stays them from drawing near to God.

CHAPTER IX

How God and the souls in Purgatory look at each other. The saint acknowledges that in speaking of these matters she cannot express herself.

All these things which I have surely in mind, in so much as in this life I have been able to understand them, are, as compared with what I have said, extreme in their greatness. Beside them, all the sights and sounds and justice and truths of this world seem to me lies and nothingness. I am left confused because I cannot find words extreme enough for these things.

I perceive there to be so much conformity between God and the soul that when He sees it in the purity in which His Divine Majesty created it He gives it a burning love, which draws it to Himself, which is strong enough to destroy it, immortal though it be, and which causes it to be so transformed in God that it sees itself as though it were none other than God. Unceasingly He draws it to Himself and breathes fire into it, never letting it go until He has led it to the state whence it came forth, that is to the pure cleanliness in which it was created. When with its inner sight the soul sees itself drawn by God with such loving fire, then it is melted by the heat of the glowing love for God, its most dear Lord, which it feels overflowing it. And it sees by the divine light that God does not cease from drawing it, nor from leading it, lovingly and with much care and unfailing foresight, to its full perfection, doing this of His pure love. But the soul, being hindered by sin, cannot go whither God draws it; it cannot follow the uniting look with which He would draw it to Himself. Again the soul perceives the grievousness of being held back from seeing the divine light; the soul's instinct too, being drawn by that uniting look, craves to be unhindered. I say that it is the sight of these things which begets in the souls the pain they feel in Purgatory. Not that they make account of their pain; most great though it be, they deem it a far less evil than to find themselves going against the will of God, whom they clearly see to be on fire with extreme and pure love for them.

Strongly and unceasingly this love draws the soul with that uniting look, as though it had nought else than this to do. Could the soul who understood find a worse

Purgatory in which to rid itself sooner of all the hindrance in its way, it would swiftly fling itself therein, driven by the conforming love between itself and God.

CHAPTER X

How God uses Purgatory to make the soul wholly pure. The soul acquires in Purgatory a purity so great that were it well for it still to stay there after it had been purged of sin, it would no longer suffer.

I see, too, certain rays and shafts of light which go out from that divine love towards the soul and are penetrating and strong enough to seem as though they must destroy not only the body but the soul too, were that possible. Two works are wrought by these rays, the first purification and the second destruction. Look at gold: the more you melt it, the better it becomes; you could melt it until you had destroyed in it every imperfection. Thus does fire work on material things. The soul cannot be destroyed in so far as it is in God, but in so far as it is in itself it can be destroyed; the more it is purified, the more is self destroyed within it, until at last it is pure in God.

When gold has been purified up to twenty-four carats, it can no longer be consumed by any fire; not gold itself but only dross can be burnt away. Thus the divine fire works in the soul: God holds the soul in the fire until its every imperfection is burnt away and it is brought to perfection, as it were to the purity of twenty-four carats, each soul however according to its own degree. When the soul has been purified it stays wholly in God, having nothing of self in it; its being is in God who has led this cleansed soul to Himself; it can suffer no more for nothing is left in it to be burnt away; were it held in the fire when it has thus been cleansed, it would feel no pain. Rather the fire of divine love would be to it like eternal life and in no way contrary to it.

CHAPTER XI

Of the desire of souls in Purgatory to be wholly cleansed of the stains of their sins. The wisdom of God who suddenly hides their faults from these souls.

The soul was created as well conditioned as it is capable of being for reaching perfection, if it live as God has ordained and does not foul itself with any stain of sin. But having fouled itself by original sin, it loses its gifts and graces and lies dead, nor can it rise again save by God's means. And when God, by baptism, has raised it from the dead, it is still prone to evil, inclining and being led to actual sin unless it resist. And thus it dies again.

Then God by another special grace raises it again, yet it stays so sullied and so turned to self that all the divine workings of which we have spoken are needed to recall it to its first state in which God created it; without them it could never get back thither. And when the soul finds itself on the road back to its first state, its need to be transformed in God kindles in it a fire so great that this is its Purgatory. Not that it can look upon this as Purgatory, but its instinct to God, aflame and thwarted, makes Purgatory.

A last act of love is done by God without help from man. So many hidden imperfections are in the soul that, did it see them, it would live in despair. But in the state of which we have spoken they are all burnt away, and only when they have gone does God shew them to the soul, so that it may see that divine working which kindles the fire of love in which its imperfections have been burnt away.

CHAPTER XII

How suffering in Purgatory is coupled with joy.

Know that what man deems perfection in himself is in God's sight faulty, for all the things a man does which he sees or feels or means or wills or remembers to have a perfect seeming are wholly fouled and sullied unless he acknowledge them to be from God. If a work is to be perfect it must be wrought in us but not chiefly by us, for God's works must be done in Him and not wrought chiefly by man.

Such works are those last wrought in us by God of His pure and clean love, by Him alone without merit of ours, and so penetrating are they and such fire do they kindle in the soul, that the body which wraps it seems to be consumed as in a furnace never to be quenched until death. It is true that love for God which fills the soul to overflowing, gives it, so I see it, a happiness beyond what can be told, but this happiness takes not one pang from the pain of the souls in Purgatory. Rather the love of these souls, finding itself hindered, causes their pain; and the more perfect is the love of which God has made them capable, the greater is their pain. So that the souls in Purgatory enjoy the greatest happiness and endure the greatest pain; the one does not hinder the other.

CHAPTER XIII

The souls in Purgatory are no longer in a state to acquire merit. How these souls look on the charity exercised for them in the world.

If the souls in Purgatory could purge themselves by contrition, they would pay all their debt in one instant, such blazing vehemence would their contrition have in the clear light shed for them on the grievousness of being hindered from reaching their end and the love of God.

Know surely that not the least farthing of payment is remitted to those souls, for thus has it been determined by God's justice. So much for what God does as for what the souls do, they can no longer choose for themselves, nor can they see or will, save as God wills, for thus has it been determined for them.

And if any alms be done them by those who are in the world to lessen the time of their pain, they cannot turn with affection to contemplate the deed, saving as it is weighed in the most just scales of the divine will. They leave all in God's hands who pays Himself as His infinite goodness pleases. If they could turn to contemplate the alms except as it is within the divine will, there would be self in what they did and they would lose sight of God's will, which would make a

Hell for them. Therefore they await immovably all that God gives them, whether pleasure and happiness or pain, and never more can they turn their eyes back to themselves.

CHAPTER XIV

Of the submission of the souls in Purgatory to God's will.

So intimate with God are the souls in Purgatory and so changed to His will, that in all things they are content with His most holy ordinance. And if a soul were brought to see God when it had still a trifle of which to purge itself, a great injury would be done it. For since pure love and supreme justice could not brook that stained soul, and to bear with its presence would not befit God, it would suffer a torment worse than ten purgatories. To see God when full satisfaction had not yet been made Him, even if the time of purgation lacked but the twinkling of an eye, would be unbearable to that soul. It would sooner go to a thousand hells, to rid itself of the little rust still clinging to it, than stand in the divine presence when it was not yet wholly cleansed.

CHAPTER XV

Reproaches which the souls in Purgatory make to people in the world.

And so that blessed soul, seeing the aforesaid things by the divine light, said: "I would fain send up a cry so loud that it would put fear in all men on the earth. I would say to them: 'Wretches, why do you let yourselves be thus blinded by the world, you whose need is so great and grievous, as you will know at the moment of death, and who make no provision for it whatsoever?"

"You have all taken shelter beneath hope in God's mercy, which is, you say, very great, but you see not that this great goodness of God will judge you for having gone against the will of so good a Lord. His goodness should constrain you to do all His will, not give you hope in ill-doing, for His justice cannot fail but in one way or another must needs be fully satisfied. "Cease to hug yourselves, saying: 'I will confess my sins and then receive plenary indulgence, and at that moment I shall be purged of all my sins and thus shall be saved.' Think of the confession and the contrition needed for that plenary indulgence, so hardly come by that, if you knew, you would tremble in great fear, more sure you would never win it than that you ever could."

CHAPTER XVI

This Soul shews again how the sufferings of the souls in Purgatory are no hindrance at all to their peace and their joy.

I see the souls suffer the pains of Purgatory having before their eyes two works of God.

First, they see themselves suffering pain willingly, and as they consider their own deserts and acknowledge how they have grieved God, it seems to them that He has shewn them great mercy, for if His goodness had not tempered justice with mercy, making satisfaction with the precious blood of Jesus Christ, one sin would deserve a thousand perpetual hells. And therefore the souls suffer pain willingly, and would not lighten it by one pang, knowing that they most fully deserve it and that it has been well ordained, and they no more complain of God, as far as their will goes, than if they were in eternal life.

The second work they see is the happiness they feel as they contemplate God's ordinance and the love and mercy with which He works on the soul.

In one instant God imprints these two sights on their minds, and because they are in grace they are aware of these sights and understand them as they are, in the measure of their capacity. Thus a great happiness is granted them which never fails; rather it grows as they draw nearer God. These souls see these sights neither in nor of themselves but in God, on whom they are far more intent than on the pains they suffer, and of whom they make far greater account, beyond all comparison, than of their pains. For every glimpse which can be had of God exceeds any pain or joy a man can feel. Albeit, however, it exceeds the pain and joy of these souls, it lessens them by not a tittle.

CHAPTER XVII

She concludes by applying all she has said of the souls in Purgatory to what she feels, and has proved in her own soul.

This form of purgation, which I see in the souls in Purgatory, I feel in my own mind. In the last two years

I have felt it most; every day I feel and see it more clearly. I see my soul within this body as in a purgatory, formed as is the true Purgatory and like it, but so measured that the body can bear with it and not die; little by little it grows until the body die.

I see my spirit estranged from all things, even things spiritual, which can feed it, such as gaiety, delight and consolation, and without the power so to enjoy anything, spiritual or temporal, by will or mind or memory, as to let me say one thing contents me more than another.

Inwardly I find myself as it were besieged. All things by which spiritual or bodily life is refreshed have, little by little, been taken from my inner self, which knows, now they are gone, that they fed and comforted. But so hateful and abhorrent are these things, as they are known to the spirit, that they all go never to return. This is because of the spirit's instinct to rid itself of whatever hinders its perfection; so ruthless is it that to fulfill its purpose it would all but cast itself into Hell. Therefore it ever deprives the inner man of all on which it can feed, besieging it so cunningly that it lets not the least atom of imperfection pass unseen and unabhorred.

As for my outer man, it too, since the spirit does not respond to it, is so besieged that it finds nothing to refresh it on the earth if it follow its human instinct. No comfort is left it save God, who works all this by love and very mercifully in satisfaction of His justice. To perceive this gives my outer man great peace and happiness, but happiness which neither lessens my pain nor weakens the siege. Yet no pain could ever be inflicted on me so great that I would wish to depart from the divine ordinance. I neither leave my prison nor seek to go forth from it: let God do what is needed! My happiness is that God be satisfied, nor could I suffer a worse pain than that of going outside God's ordinance, so just I see Him to be and so very merciful.

All these things of which I have spoken are what I see and, as it were, touch, but I cannot find fit words to say as much as I would of them. Nor can I say rightly what I have told of the work done in me, which I have felt spiritually. I have told it however.

The prison in which I seem to myself to be is the world, my chains the body, and it is my soul enlightened by grace which knows the grievousness of being held down or kept back and thus hindered from pursuing its end. This gives my soul great pain for it is very tender. By God's grace it receives a certain dignity which makes it like unto God; nay, rather He lets it share His goodness so that it becomes one with Him. And since it is impossible that God suffer pain, this immunity too befalls the souls who draw near Him; the nearer they come to Him, the more they partake of what is His.

Therefore to be hindered on its way, as it is, causes the soul unbearable pain. The pain and the hindrance wrest it from its first natural state, which by grace is revealed to it, and finding itself deprived of what it is able to receive, it suffers a pain more or less great according to the measure of its esteem for God. The more the soul knows God, the more it esteems Him and the more sinless it becomes, so that the hindrance in its way grows yet more terrible to it, above all because the soul which is unhindered and wholly recollected in God knows Him as He truly is.

As the man who would let himself be killed rather than offend God feels death and its pain, but is given by the light of God a zeal which causes him to rate divine honor above bodily death, so the soul who knows God's ordinance rates it above all possible inner and outer torments, terrible though they may be, for this is a work of God who surpasses all that can be felt or imagined. Moreover God when He occupies a soul, in however small a degree, keeps it wholly busied over His Majesty so that nothing else counts for it. Thus it loses all which is its own, and can of itself neither see nor speak nor know loss or pain. But, as I have already said clearly, it knows all in one instant when it leaves this life.

Finally and in conclusion, let us understand that God who is best and greatest causes all that is of man to be lost, and that Purgatory cleanses it away.

END

Note: Revelation vs. Spiritism

Revelation

God can reveal the future to his prophets or to other saints. Still, a sound Christian attitude consists in putting oneself confidently into the hands of Providence for whatever concerns the future, and giving up all unhealthy curiosity about it. (*Catechism of the Catholic Church*, no. 2115)

The Church does not deny that, with a special permission of God, the souls of the departed may appear to the living, and even manifest things unknown to the latter. But, understood as the art or science of evoking the dead, necromancy is held by theologians to be due to the agency of evil spirits, for the means taken are inadequate to produce the expected results. In pretended evocations of the dead, there may be many things explainable naturally or due to fraud; how much is real, and how much must be attributed to imagination and deception, cannot be determined, but real facts of necromancy, with the use of incantations and magical rites, are looked upon by theologians, after St. Thomas, II-II, Q. xcv, aa. iii, iv, as special modes of divination, due to demoniacal intervention, and divination itself is a form of superstition. (*Catholic Encyclopedia, 1913, edited by Charles G. Herbermann, et. al.*)

The Danger of Occultism

(Excerpt from Fr. Gabriele Amorth, Exorcist, President, International Association of Exorcists):

Spiritism is the evocation of the dead through a medium. The medium is a type of . . . channel or means of communication with the spiritual world, in order to learn hidden things or to know the fate of a dearly departed. There are, in fact, many — unilluminated by Christian faith — who, at the death of a dear person or in the unrestrained desire to know the future, turn, out of desperation, to mediums, often with inauspicious effects on their lives...

Also here, as in magic, there are many braggarts who look to make money at the expense of those who are suffering. But there are also many mediums who are truly able to get in contact with spiritual entities. These presumed spirits of the dead often reveal things that are unknown to the medium himself but are known to the client, who, once conquered by the credibility of the "voice," does not hesitate to believe all the other revelations in future sessions. Often these voices announce beautiful things or leave edifying messages that are difficult to ignore. In brief, spiritism in these cases seems to work, and it draws many followers.

The fact, then, that they are able to obtain information about events that have truly happened and are unknown to the medium leads us to attribute these communications to an intelligent external cause — that is, to spirits. But of what exactly are we speaking?...

But first let us see what the Church says on the topic...

All forms of divination are to be rejected: recourse to Satan or demons, conjuring up the dead or other practices falsely supposed to "unveil the future." Consulting horoscopes, astrology, palm reading, interpretation of omens and lots; the phenomena of clairvoyance, and recourse to mediums all conceal a desire for power over time, history, and, in the last analysis, other human beings, as well as a wish to conciliate hidden powers. They contradict the honor, respect, and loving fear that we owe to God alone. (CCC, no. 2116)

In light of this and of my long exorcistical practice, I believe that the evoked, presumed souls of the deceased (those that in precedence I called "roaming" or "wandering") are in reality unclean, awakened spirits, attracted, indeed "forced," by the evocation to manifest themselves. I also believe that to lead or simply to assist at such practices, even only occasionally, besides being a mortal sin, can provoke concrete and serious harm to the person. My agenda is full of appointments given to those who have consulted a medium. These individuals tell me that after such experiences, even long after, their problems increase: they have difficulty sleeping; they perceive some strange presences in their ambiences; they find it difficult to study; they experience a growing desire to commit suicide; they develop an unexplainable hatred toward others, and they become besieged by obsessive thoughts. Unfortunately the list could be lengthened to include the risks of contracting a serious spiritual evil such as a diabolical possession. The correlation between the cause and the diagnosis is so frequent that it is difficult for me to think that spiritism has nothing to do with the demon. The fact is, and I base this on the experience of all my colleagues in this ministry, that these evils are curable only through the medicine of the spirit: exorcism, blessings, prayer, and the sacraments; and this leads to the confirmation of all that I have said.

The original in Italian:

Lo spiritismo o negromanzia (dal greco *necròs* = morto e *manzia*= divinazione) – attività di comune pratica nelle culture tradizionali, soprattutto africane e sudamericane, e molto diffusa in Occidente a partire da metà '800 – è l'evocazione dei defunti attraverso un medium. Il medium, a sua volta, è una sorta di "sacerdote" dello spiritismo (alla stessa stregua per cui un mago è il "sacerdote" del rito magico), che funge da "canale" verso il mondo degli spiriti, per apprendere cose nascoste o per conoscere il destino del "caro estinto". Ci sono, infatti, molte persone che, alla morte di una persona cara o nel desiderio sfrenato di conoscere il futuro, prese dalla disperazione e certo non illuminate dalla fede cristiana, si rivolgono ai sensitivi (un secondo modo con cui chiamare i medium), con effetti spesso nefasti sulle loro vite. . .

Naturalmente anche qui, come nella magia, ci sono tanti fanfaroni che cercano di far soldi a spese di chi è nella sofferenza. Ma ci sono anche tanti medium che "funzionano", cioè che sono realmente in grado di mettersi in contatto con queste entità spirituali. Con essi non di rado accade che le presunte "anime dei defunti" rivelino cose sconosciute al medium stesso e note invece al cliente, che, una volta conquistato dalla credibilità della "voce", non esita a credere a tutte le altre "rivelazioni" nelle sedute successive. Spesso le "voci" annunciano cose belle, lanciano messaggi edificanti a cui è difficile non dare retta. Insomma, lo spiritismo in questo caso sembra proprio funzionare! Sarà anche per questo che tira molto.

Il fatto, poi, che si possano ottenere informazioni di fatti realmente accaduti e sconosciuti al medium ci inducono ad attribuire queste comunicazioni a una causa intelligente esterna, cioè a degli spiriti. Ma di cosa stiamo parlando esattamente? . . .

Prima però vediamo cosa dice in proposito la Chiesa...

"Tutte le forme di divinazione sono da respingere: ricorso a Satana o ai demoni, evocazione dei morti o altre pratiche che a torto si ritiene che "svelino" l'avvenire. La consultazione degli oroscopi, l'astrologia, la chiromanzia, l'interpretazione dei presagi e delle sorti, i fenomeni di veggenza, il ricorso ai medium manifestano una volontà di dominio sul tempo, sulla storia ed infine sugli uomini ed insieme un desiderio di rendersi propizie le potenze nascoste. Sono in contraddizione con l'onore e il rispetto, congiunto a timore amante, che dobbiamo a Dio solo".

Alla luce di questo e della mia lunga pratica esorcistica, confermo che le presunte anime dei defunti evocate (quelle che in precedenza avevo chiamato "vaganti") siano in realtà spiriti immondi risvegliati, richiamati, anzi "costretti" dall'evocazione a manifestarsi. Ritengo che condurre o semplicemente assistere a tali pratiche, anche solo occasionalmente, oltre che essere un peccato mortale, possa provocare concreti e gravi danni allo spirito. La mia agenda è piena di appuntamenti dati a persone che si sono rivolte ai medium. Queste mi raccontano che dopo tali esperienze, anche a distanza di molto tempo, è aumentato il loro disagio: da difficoltà nel sonno alla percezione di "presenze" estranee nei loro ambienti, dalla difficoltà a studiare a un desiderio crescente di suicidarsi, da un odio inspiegabile verso gli altri a improvvisi pensieri ossessivi. E la lista sarebbe lunga e comprende, purtroppo, anche il rischio di contrarre un grave male spirituale, la possessione diabolica. La correlazione tra la causa e la diagnosi mi sembra così frequente che risulta difficile pensare che lo spiritismo non abbia a che fare con il demonio. Il fatto poi che, e qui mi baso anche sull'esperienza di tanti miei colleghi esorcisti, questi mali siano curabili solo attraverso le "medicine dello spirito" – esorcismo, benedizioni, preghiera, sacramenti – mi induce a confermare quanto detto.

Caritas Publishing brings you spiritual
riches of the Holy Roman Catholic Tradition
at the most affordable prices possible.
caritaspublishing.com